LAND O LAKES

DINNER
tonight!

pasta — chicken — grilling

CREATIVE
PUBLISHING
international

MINNETONKA, MINNESOTA

Publisher: Pete Theisen
Director of Test Kitchens: Lydia Botham
Editor: Mary Sue Peterson
Assistant Editor: Cindy Manwarren

For questions regarding recipes in this cookbook or Land O'Lakes
products, call 1-800-328-4155 or visit us at our Web site at:
http://www.landolakes.com

President/CEO: David D. Murphy
Vice President/Editorial: Patricia K. Jacobsen
Vice President/Retail Sales & Marketing: Richard M. Miller

Executive Editor: Elaine Perry
Project Manager: Linnéa Christensen
Senior Art Director: Stephanie Michaud
Executive Food Editor: Carol Frieberg
Desktop Publishing Specialist: Laurie Kristensen
Publishing Production Manager: Kim Gerber

Pictured on front cover: Pasta with Fresh Tomatoes (page 54).

Recipes developed and tested by the Land O'Lakes Test Kitchens.

Printed on American paper by:
  R. R. Donnelley & Sons Co.
10 9 8 7 6 5 4 3 2 1

Creative Publishing international, Inc.
5900 Green Oak Drive
Minnetonka, Minnesota 55343
Printed in U.S.A.
For book inquiries, call 1-800-328-3895

Library of Congress Cataloging-in-Publication Data
Dinner tonight! : pasta, chicken, grilling / Land O'Lakes.
     p. cm.
   Includes index.
   ISBN 0-86573-871-8
   1. Cookery (Pasta) 2. Dinner and dining. I. Land O'Lakes, Inc.

TX809.M17 D564 2000
641.5--dc21   99-047730

introduction

If "What's for dinner?" is a common question at your house, you will appreciate and treasure this cookbook. Inside you'll find everything from easy skillet casseroles to roasted herb chicken to lamb chops on the grill. The kids will love the picnic drumsticks and grilled stuffed cheeseburgers. And someday you may even try your hand at homemade pasta.

The best part about these recipes is that they are as easy to love as they are to prepare. Each recipe has prep and cook times included to help you plan ahead and organize your meal preparation. In addition, each recipe is photographed in full color to help you choose the perfect meal!

Plus, these are recipes you can depend on. Each recipe has been tested by the professional home economists in our Test Kitchens. We've put the recipes in an easy-to-read, easy-to-follow format to help you put dinner on the table with minimal stress and maximum satisfaction!

We believe that Land O'Lakes is a name cooks have learned to trust for quality. We are proud to offer you this collection of some of our favorite recipes and wish you much success as you share them with your friends and family. May *Dinner Tonight* truly make you proud!

Popular Kitchen Herbs

Used appropriately, herbs can transform a simple dish into a delightful experience of savory, spicy, tangy and piquant flavors.

Basil: *its fresh leaf has a sweet, clovelike spiciness that increases with cooking. Basil combines well with garlic, tomatoes and mushrooms, which makes it an Italian favorite.*

Bay Leaf: *frequently used to make bouquet garnish, marinades, stocks, pates, stuffing and curries. Bay is one herb that is better dried than fresh. Added at the beginning of cooking, the leaf is removed before serving.*

Chives: *chopped and sprinkled on at the end of cooking, chives add a mild onion flavor to soups, salads, chicken, potatoes and more. Blend with butter, cream cheeese, sour cream and sauces. Chives freeze well but are poor dried.*

Cilanto (coriander): *these leaves have a spicy, lemony, pungent flavor that balances perfectly with hot, spicy foods. The potency decreases with cooking. Coriander seeds add an aromatic lift to chutney, curries and vegetables.*

Dill: *the spicy, lemony taste of dill is totally unique. Whole seeds are added to pickles, potato salads, soups and salmon. The leaves enhance both cold and hot sauces, vegetable dips, salads and fish.*

Mint: *has a clean, sharp bite and can be used individually or blended. It adds a refreshing twist to salads and vegetables. It also blends smoothly with chocolate in cakes and desserts. The dainty, delicate leaves are ideal for garnishing.*

Marjoram: *the mild, savory flavor is suitable for tomato dishes, pastas, poultry, meat, fish and vegetables. This herb dries well but is best when added toward the end of cooking.*

Oregano: *has a zesty flavor slightly stronger than marjoram. Its aromatic appeal is a favorite in Italian dishes like pizza, spaghetti and lasagna. It also enhances salads, meat and egg dishes.*

Parsley: *one of the most popular kitchen herbs. Its bright green leaves and mild taste enhance the flavor of other foods and herbs. Use in soups, sauces, salads, dressings, egg dishes and more. Flat leafed Italian parsley and curly parsley both make colorful garnishes.*

Chicken Basics

Purchasing Chicken:

Chicken is popular today, not only because it is nutritious and low in fat, but also because its delicate flavor blends well with many herbs and spices. In addition, chicken is an economical buy at the supermarket.

When purchasing chicken, look for a plump-bodied, blemish-free, smooth-skinned bird.

Allow about $1/2$ pound (8 ounces) bone-in, skin-on chicken per serving. For boneless, skinless chicken plan about $1/4$ pound (4 ounces) per serving. Whole chickens are usually the best buy; the bigger the bird, the more meat in proportion to bone. Chicken can also be purchased in a variety of cuts. Here are some of the different cuts of chicken you will find:

Whole Roasting Chickens are larger and older birds. They weigh between 4 and 5 pounds and are excellent for stuffing and roasting.

Broilers - Fryers are the most common type of chicken. The birds are young and weigh between 3 and 4 pounds.

Quartered Chickens are cut into four pieces with wing attached to breast and leg attached to thigh.

Chicken Pieces consist of a whole chicken cut into eight pieces—two legs, two thighs, two wings and the breast split into two pieces. Sometimes the back and giblets are included.

Chicken Breasts can be purchased whole, with or without ribs attached; split, with or without the ribs; or boneless. All forms can be purchased skin-on or skinless.

Chicken Thighs, Legs and Wings come in a variety of package sizes and should be purchased according to the number of servings needed.

Storing Chicken:

Proper storage of poultry is essential to maintain flavor and quality. Poultry may be kept safely in the refrigerator for up to two days and in the freezer for six months. Wash poultry in cold water, pat dry and wrap in plastic food wrap or aluminum foil for refrigeration. If stored in freezer, wash in cold water, pat dry and wrap in freezer paper, aluminum foil or plastic food freezer bags. The freezer temperature should be 0°F or less.

To Thaw Frozen Chicken:

The safest way to thaw chicken is in the refrigerator. Thawing a whole 4 to 5-pound bird takes 1 to 2 days. Thawing a cup-up chicken takes 4 to 9 hours. If desired, chicken can be thawed in cold water. In large bowl, cover chicken with cold water; change water every 30 minutes to keep water cold.

Chicken defrosted in the microwave should be cooked immediately after thawing because some areas of the food may become warm and begin to cook during microwaving. Holding partially cooked food is not recommended because any bacteria present wouldn't have been destroyed. **Foods defrosted in the microwave or by the cold water method should be cooked before refreezing.**

Tips on Grilling

Grills

Many types of grills are available. Many sizes, shapes and price ranges are offered. Determine cooking objectives before deciding on the type to purchase.

- Charcoal grills (large size and portable or tabletop)
- Brazier or open grill
- Round covered kettle
- Rectangular or square cooker with a hinged lid
- Gas or electric grill
- Smokers

Fuel

Charcoal briquettes are most commonly used for grilling. All recipes in this cookbook were tested using charcoal briquettes and a gas grill. Other fuels available include:

- Hardwood charcoal (made directly from whole pieces of wood--no additives or fillers)
- Mesquite
- Wood
- Smoking or flavor chips

Each type of fuel imparts a unique flavor to the cooked food.

To determine the number of charcoal briquettes needed, spread a single layer of charcoal briquettes 1 inch beyond the edge of the food for small cuts of meat. For longer-cooking foods, use additional charcoal briquettes in a pyramid shape to provide proper ventilation. For indirect heating, use the same number of coals as for direct heating. Once pushed to the side, they will layer up to four coals deep.

Ignite briquettes 30 to 40 minutes before you intend to cook. Be sure to open any vents on the grill. Light and preheat gas grills according to the manufacturer's directions, usually about 15 minutes. Be sure to keep the hood up when lighting a gas grill. For indirect grilling on a dual control gas grill, use single control, opposite meat placement.

Direct & Indirect Heating

The **direct** cooking method means to place the food on the grill directly over the coals. It is faster, since more intense heat is provided. Faster-cooking meats or thin pieces of meat, poultry or fish are usually grilled over direct heat.

The **indirect** cooking method means to place the food on the grill to the side opposite the coals. It is a slower cooking method because less heat is provided. This minimizes flare-ups if dripping occurs. It is recommended when sugary sauces, glazes or marinades are applied. It also is used for large pieces of poultry, meat, fish or fatty foods to achieve more even cooking.

favorite Pasta!

Spicy Spaghetti Sauce with
Pepperoni and Homemade Pasta

Homemade Pasta

Homemade pasta can be made with or without a pasta machine or food processor.

Preparation time: 1 hour • Standing time: 20 minutes • Cooking time: 3 minutes (pictured on page 10)

2 to 2 1/3 cups all-purpose
    flour
1/8 teaspoon salt
1/3 cup water
2 eggs
1 teaspoon olive <u>or</u>
    vegetable oil

3 quarts (12 cups) water
1 teaspoon salt

In large bowl combine 2 cups flour and 1/8 teaspoon salt. In small bowl, with fork, beat together 1/3 cup water, eggs and oil. Stir egg mixture into flour until dough forms. Turn dough onto floured surface. Knead, sprinkling with remaining 1/3 cup flour as needed to prevent sticking, until dough is smooth and elastic (8 to 10 minutes). Divide dough into quarters. On lightly floured surface roll each quarter into 12-inch square, about 1/16-inch thick. Very lightly sprinkle each square with flour. Let stand 20 minutes. Cut as desired (thin strips, wide strips, squares, etc.).* To cook pasta, in Dutch oven bring 3 quarts water and 1 teaspoon salt to a full boil. Slowly add desired amount of pasta. Cook in boiling water until tender but still firm (2 to 3 minutes).
YIELD: 1 pound (8 servings).

<u>Food Processor Directions:</u> In food processor bowl with metal blade combine flour and 1/8 teaspoon salt. Add eggs and oil. Process with on/off pulses until dough resembles coarse crumbs (30 to 40 seconds). Slowly add water through feed tube while processor is running. Process until dough pulls away from sides of bowl (1 to 2 minutes). If dough is sticky, add 1 tablespoon at a time of remaining 1/3 cup flour, processing with on/off pulses until flour is incorporated into dough. Divide dough into quarters. Continue as directed above.

<u>Pasta Machine Directions:</u> Prepare, knead and divide dough as directed above. Pass each quarter of dough through pasta machine according to manufactures' directions until pasta is about 1/16-inch thick. Continue as directed above.

*At this point, pasta can be dried for about 1 hour, then stored in an airtight container and refrigerated for up to 3 days. Or dry pasta for about 1 hour, seal in freezer bags or freezer container and store in freezer up to 8 months.

Nutrition Information (1 serving): Calorie 140, Protein 5g; Carbohydrate 24g; Fat 2g; Cholesterol 55mg; Sodium 50mg.

Spicy Spaghetti Sauce *with* Pepperoni

*A chunky spaghetti sauce that's ready when you are
and brimming with flavor.*

Preparation time: 10 minutes • Cooking time: 25 minutes (pictured on page 10)

1 cup sliced 1/2-inch fresh
  mushrooms

2 medium (1 cup) onions,
  chopped

1 cup pitted ripe olives,
  sliced 1/2-inch

1/2 cup chopped fresh parsley

1 cup water

2 (14 1/2-ounce) cans stewed
  tomatoes

1 (6-ounce) can tomato paste

2 teaspoons dried basil leaves

1/2 teaspoon dried oregano
  leaves

1/4 teaspoon pepper

1 tablespoon country-style
  Dijon mustard

1 teaspoon finely chopped
  fresh garlic

8 ounces uncooked dried
  spaghetti

3 ounces sliced pepperoni

In 3-quart saucepan combine all ingredients <u>except</u> spaghetti and pepperoni. Cook over medium heat, stirring occasionally, until sauce is thickened (15 to 20 minutes). Meanwhile, cook spaghetti according to package directions. Drain. Stir pepperoni into sauce; continue cooking until heated through (4 to 5 minutes). Serve over hot cooked spaghetti. **YIELD:** 6 servings.

Nutrition Information (1 serving): Calories 300; Protein 10g; Carbohydrate 44g; Fat 10g; Cholesterol 10mg; Sodium 980mg.

Red Tomato Sauce *with* Meatballs

*Try this traditional family favorite
of spaghetti and meatballs.*

Preparation time: 45 minutes • Cooking time: 3 hours

Sauce

5 cups water

2 (12-ounce) cans tomato paste

1 medium (1/2 cup) onion,
  chopped

1 (29-ounce) can tomato puree

3 tablespoons chopped fresh
  oregano leaves*

1 tablespoon chopped fresh
  basil leaves**

2 teaspoons sugar

1 teaspoon salt

1 bay leaf

1 teaspoon finely chopped
  fresh garlic

Meatballs

1/2 cup dry Italian bread
  crumbs

1/2 cup freshly grated
  Parmesan cheese

1/2 pound bulk Italian sausage

1/2 pound ground beef

2 eggs

1/4 teaspoon coarsely ground
  pepper

1/2 teaspoon finely chopped
  fresh garlic

1 tablespoon olive <u>or</u>
  vegetable oil

1 (8-ounce) package uncooked
  dried spaghetti

In Dutch oven combine water and tomato paste. Stir with wire whisk until smooth. Add all remaining sauce ingredients. Cook over medium high heat, stirring occasionally, until sauce just comes to a boil (6 to 8 minutes). Cover; reduce heat to low. Continue cooking, stirring occasionally, until sauce is thickened (1 1/2 to 2 hours). Meanwhile, in large bowl combine all meatball ingredients <u>except</u> oil and spaghetti; mix well. Form into 16 meatballs. In 10-inch skillet heat oil; add meatballs. Cook over medium heat, turning occasionally, until well browned (10 to 12 minutes). Drain meatballs; stir into sauce. Cover loosely; continue cooking over low heat, stirring occasionally, 1 hour. Remove bay leaf. Meanwhile, cook spaghetti according to package directions. Drain. Serve sauce and meatballs over hot cooked spaghetti.
YIELD: 8 servings.

*1 tablespoon dried oregano leaves can be substituted for 3 tablespoons chopped fresh oregano leaves.

**1 teaspoon dried basil leaves can be substituted for 1 tablespoon chopped fresh basil leaves.

TIP: Chopped ripe tomato, sliced mushrooms, sliced black olives or chopped green pepper can be added to sauce during last hour of cooking.

*Nutrition Information (1 serving): Calories 410; Protein 21g; Carbohydrate 55g; Fat 14g;
Cholesterol 85mg; Sodium 1740mg.*

ABC Vegetables 'N Chili

Kids will love this hearty
pasta soup.

Preparation time: 10 minutes • Cooking time: 1 hour 10 minutes

1 medium (1/2 cup) onion,
  chopped
1 pound lean ground beef
3 cups water
1 (15-ounce) can tomato sauce
1 (14 1/2-ounce) can stewed
  tomatoes, cut up
1 to 2 teaspoons chili powder
1 teaspoon salt
1/4 teaspoon pepper
2 cups frozen mixed vegetable
  combination
1 cup uncooked dried alphabet-
  shaped pasta <u>or</u> pasta rings

LAND O LAKES® Cheddar
  Cheese, shredded, if
  desired

In Dutch oven combine onion and ground beef. Cook over medium high heat, stirring occasionally, until beef is browned (10 to 15 minutes); drain off fat. Return beef to Dutch oven. Add water, tomato sauce, stewed tomatoes, chili powder, salt and pepper. Continue cooking, stirring occasionally, until chili just comes to a boil (10 to 15 minutes). Add vegetable combination and pasta. Continue cooking, stirring occasionally, until chili just comes to a boil (5 to 10 minutes). Reduce heat to medium low. Continue cooking, stirring often, 20 to 30 minutes or until flavors are blended. Sprinkle cheese over individual bowls of chili. **YIELD:** 8 servings.

Nutrition Information (1 serving): Calories 210; Protein 14g; Carbohydrate 23g; Fat 8g; Cholesterol 36mg; Sodium 770mg.

Sausage 'N Pasta Stew

*Tomatoes, pasta, sausage and beans combine in
this hearty stew.*

Preparation time: 20 minutes • Cooking time: 36 minutes

1/4 cup chopped onion

3/4 pound sliced 1/2-inch
Italian sausage links

1/2 teaspoon finely chopped
fresh garlic

1 cup water

2 (28-ounce) cans whole
tomatoes, undrained, cut up

2 teaspoons sugar

1/2 teaspoon Italian herb
seasoning*

3 ounces (1 cup) uncooked
dried rotini (corkscrew <u>or</u>
pasta twists)

2 cups frozen cut broccoli

1 (15-ounce) can Great
Northern beans, rinsed,
drained.

Freshly grated Parmesan
cheese, if desired

In Dutch oven cook onion, sausage and garlic over medium high heat until sausage is browned (8 to 10 minutes); drain off fat. Add water, tomatoes, sugar and Italian herb seasoning. Continue cooking until mixture comes to a full boil (6 to 8 minutes); stir in rotini. Reduce heat to medium. Continue cooking, stirring occasionally, until rotini is tender (8 to 11 minutes). Stir in broccoli and beans. Continue cooking, stirring occasionally, until broccoli is crisply tender (5 to 7 minutes). Serve with Parmesan cheese. **YIELD:** 6 servings.

*1/8 teaspoon each dried oregano leaves, dried marjoram leaves and dried basil leaves and 1/16 teaspoon rubbed sage can be substituted for 1/2 teaspoon Italian herb seasoning.

*Nutrition Information (1 serving): Calories 230; Protein 13g; Carbohydrate 28g; Fat 8g;
Cholesterol 22mg; Sodium 470mg.*

Skillet Pizza Casserole

Your family will love this skillet dinner with
all-time favorite pizza flavors.

Preparation time: 20 minutes • Cooking time: 25 minutes

4 ounces (2 cups) uncooked
   dried egg noodles
1/2 pound bulk mild Italian
   sausage
1/4 cup chopped green pepper
1 medium (1/2 cup) onion,
   chopped
1/2 cup coarsely chopped
   pepperoni
1/4 cup sliced 1/4-inch ripe
   olives
1 (15-ounce) can pizza sauce
1 cup (4 ounces)
   LAND O LAKES®
   Mozzarella Cheese,
   shredded

Cook noodles according to package directions. Drain. Set aside. Meanwhile, in 10-inch skillet combine sausage, green pepper and onion. Cook over medium high heat, stirring occasionally, until sausage is browned (8 to 10 minutes). Drain off fat. Stir in noodles and all remaining ingredients <u>except</u> cheese. Continue cooking, stirring occasionally, until mixture is heated through (10 to 15 minutes). Sprinkle with cheese. Cover; let stand 3 minutes or until cheese is melted. **YIELD:** 4 servings.

TIP: To do ahead, prepare as directed above; place in greased 1 1/2-quart casserole. Cover; refrigerate. Bake at 350° for 40 to 45 minutes or until heated through. Sprinkle with cheese. Cover; let stand 3 minutes or until cheese is melted.

Nutrition Information (1 serving): Calories 420; Protein 21g; Carbohydrate 28g; Fat 24g; Cholesterol 70mg; Sodium 1440mg.

Angel Hair Spaghetti *with* Vegetables & Ham

*A wonderful combination of pasta, vegetables and ham
in a light, flavorful sauce.*

Preparation time: 20 minutes • Cooking time: 7 minutes

8 ounces uncooked dried
    angel hair pasta (very thin
    spaghetti)

1 (16-ounce) package frozen
    broccoli, carrot and
    cauliflower combination

2 tablespoons
    LAND O LAKES® Butter

1 teaspoon finely chopped
    fresh garlic

2 tablespoons all-purpose flour

1 1/4 cups milk

1 cup LAND O LAKES®
    Light Sour Cream

1 teaspoon instant chicken
    bouillon granules

1/2 teaspoon dry mustard

1/2 teaspoon dried basil
    leaves

8 ounces cooked ham, cut into
    julienne strips

Freshly grated Parmesan
    cheese

Cook pasta according to package directions. Drain. Meanwhile, cook frozen vegetables according to package directions; drain. Meanwhile, in 2-quart saucepan melt butter until sizzling; add garlic. Cook over medium low heat, stirring constantly, until garlic is tender (30 to 60 seconds). Stir in flour until smooth and bubbly (1 minute). Add all remaining ingredients <u>except</u> pasta, vegetables, ham and Parmesan cheese. Cook, stirring occasionally, until sauce is thickened (4 to 6 minutes). Remove from heat; stir in vegetables and ham. Serve over hot cooked pasta; sprinkle with Parmesan cheese.
YIELD: 8 servings.

*Nutrition Information (1 serving): Calories 250; Protein 13g; Carbohydrate 31g; Fat 8g;
Cholesterol 30mg; Sodium 480mg.*

Green & White Fettuccine

*For a fast and delicious dinner, toss fettuccine with
ham strips and peas.*

Preparation time: 20 minutes • Cooking time: 14 minutes

4 ounces uncooked dried
  fettuccine

4 ounces uncooked dried
  spinach fettuccine

1/2 cup LAND O LAKES®
  Butter

1/2 teaspoon finely chopped
  fresh garlic

1/4 cup chopped fresh parsley

1 cup whipping cream

1 (10-ounce) package frozen
  peas, thawed

1/4 teaspoon pepper

3/4 cup freshly grated
  Parmesan cheese

8 ounces cooked ham, cut
  into julienne strips

Freshly grated Parmesan
  cheese

In 4-quart saucepan cook both kinds of fettuccine according to
package directions. Drain. Set aside. In same pan melt butter
until sizzling; add garlic. Cook over medium heat, stirring occasionally, until tender (2 to 3 minutes). Stir in parsley, whipping
cream, peas and pepper. Continue cooking, stirring occasionally,
until heated through (4 to 5 minutes). Stir in both fettuccine,
3/4 cup Parmesan cheese and ham. Continue cooking, stirring
occasionally, until heated through and cheese is melted (4 to
6 minutes). Serve with additional Parmesan cheese.

YIELD: 4 servings.

*Nutrition Information (1 serving): Calories 720; Protein 31g; Carbohydrate 52g; Fat 43g;
Cholesterol 155mg; Sodium 1250mg.*

Country Pasta *with* Mozzarella

*A hearty, home-style pasta filled with bacon,
broccoli and Mozzarella cheese.*

Preparation time: 15 minutes • Cooking time: 18 minutes

8 ounces uncooked rigatoni

8 slices bacon, cut into 1-inch
pieces

2 cups broccoli flowerets

1/2 teaspoon finely chopped
fresh garlic

2 cups (8 ounces)
LAND O LAKES®
Mozzarella Cheese,
shredded

1/4 cup grated Parmesan
cheese

1/8 teaspoon ground red
pepper

1/4 cup chopped fresh parsley

Cook rigatoni according to package directions. Drain. Set aside.
Meanwhile, in 10-inch skillet cook bacon over medium high
heat, stirring occasionally, until bacon is crisp (6 to 8 minutes).
Reduce heat to medium. Add broccoli and garlic. Cook, stirring
occasionally, until broccoli is crisply tender (4 to 5 minutes).
Add rigatoni, Mozzarella cheese, Parmesan cheese and ground
red pepper. Continue cooking, stirring occasionally, until cheese
is melted (3 to 5 minutes). Sprinkle with parsley.
YIELD: 6 servings.

*Nutrition Information (1 serving): Calories 320; Protein 20g; Carbohydrate 30g; Fat 13g;
Cholesterol 30mg; Sodium 420mg.*

German Skillet Pasta

*This pasta side dish is reminiscent
of German potato salad.*

Preparation time: 15 minutes • Cooking time: 12 minutes

4 1/2 ounces (1 1/4 cups)
    uncooked dried tri-colored
    wagon wheel pasta
4 slices bacon, cut into 1-inch
    pieces
2 tablespoons sugar
1 tablespoon all-purpose flour
1/8 teaspoon salt
1/8 teaspoon pepper
1 tablespoon country-style
    Dijon mustard
1/3 cup water
1/4 cup vinegar
1/2 cup sliced 1/4-inch celery
1/4 cup chopped onion
1 tablespoon chopped fresh
    parsley

Cook pasta according to package directions. Drain. Meanwhile, in 10-inch skillet cook bacon over medium high heat until crisp (2 to 3 minutes). Reduce heat to medium. Stir in sugar, flour, salt, pepper and mustard. Continue cooking, stirring constantly, 1 minute. Add water and vinegar. Continue cooking, stirring constantly, until mixture just comes to a boil and thickens (2 to 4 minutes). Stir in pasta, celery and onion. Continue cooking, stirring occasionally, until heated through (2 to 4 minutes). Sprinkle with parsley. **YIELD:** 6 servings.

Nutrition Information (1 serving): Calories 130; Protein 4g; Carbohydrate 22g; Fat 3g; Cholesterol 5mg; Sodium 150mg.

Chicken & Peppers *with* Pasta

The fresh taste of tarragon gives this pasta toss a delicious savory flavor.

Preparation time: 30 minutes • Cooking time: 17 minutes

6 tablespoons
   LAND O LAKES® Butter
1 medium onion, cut into thin
   wedges
1 medium red pepper, cut
   into strips
1 medium yellow pepper, cut
   into strips
1 teaspoon finely chopped
   fresh garlic
3 (12 ounces each) whole
   boneless chicken breasts,
   halved, skinned, cut into
   3x1/2-inch strips
1 tablespoon finely chopped
   fresh tarragon leaves*
3/4 teaspoon salt
1/4 teaspoon coarsely ground
   pepper
8 ounces uncooked dried
   vermicelli
1 cup (4 ounces)
   LAND O LAKES®
   Mozzarella Cheese,
   shredded
1/2 cup freshly grated
   Parmesan cheese
3/4 cup half-and-half

In 12-inch skillet melt butter until sizzling; stir in onion, peppers and garlic. Cook over medium high heat until peppers are crisply tender (2 to 3 minutes). Remove vegetables from skillet with slotted spoon; set aside, <u>reserving juices in pan</u>. Add chicken, tarragon, salt and pepper to juices in pan. Continue cooking, stirring occasionally, until chicken is lightly browned and fork tender (7 to 9 minutes). Meanwhile, cook vermicelli according to package directions. Drain. Add vegetables, Mozzarella cheese, Parmesan cheese and half-and-half to chicken mixture. Reduce heat to medium; continue cooking until cheese is melted (3 to 5 minutes). Add hot cooked vermicelli; toss gently to coat. **YIELD:** 6 servings.

*1 teaspoon dried tarragon leaves can be substituted for 1 tablespoon fresh tarragon leaves.

Nutrition Information (1 serving): Calories 470; Protein 31g; Carbohydrate 33g; Fat 23g; Cholesterol 110mg; Sodium 690mg.

Chicken Lasagna

Feta cheese imparts a rich, tangy flavor to this luscious lasagna.

Preparation time: 45 minutes • Baking time: 50 minutes • Standing time: 10 minutes

Noodles

8 ounces (10) uncooked dried
  lasagna noodles

Meat Layer

1/2 pound bulk Italian sausage

2 medium (1 cup) onions,
  chopped

2 medium (2 cups) zucchini, cut
  into 1/4-inch slices, halved

1 (8-ounce) package (2 cups)
  fresh mushrooms, sliced

1/3 cup water

1 (14 1/2-ounce) can stewed
  tomatoes, cut up, <u>reserve
  liquid</u>

1 (6-ounce) can tomato paste

1 tablespoon Italian herb
  seasoning*

1 teaspoon sugar

1 teaspoon garlic salt

1/4 teaspoon pepper

2 cups cubed 1/2-inch cooked
  chicken

Filling

1/4 cup chopped fresh parsley

1 cup crumbled feta cheese

1 (15-ounce) container ricotta
  cheese**

1 egg, slightly beaten

2 cups (8 ounces)
  LAND O LAKES®
  Mozzarella Cheese,
  shredded

Heat oven to 350°. Cook lasagna noodles according to package directions. Drain. Meanwhile, in 10-inch skillet cook sausage and onions over medium high heat until sausage is brown and onions are tender (8 to 10 minutes); drain off fat. Add zucchini and mushrooms. Cook over medium heat, stirring occasionally, until vegetables are crisply tender (6 to 7 minutes). Stir in water, stewed tomatoes and reserved liquid, tomato paste, Italian herb seasoning, sugar, garlic salt and pepper. Stir in cooked chicken. In small bowl stir together all filling ingredients <u>except</u> Mozzarella cheese. Arrange <u>half</u> of noodles in greased 13x9-inch baking pan. Spread with <u>half</u> of filling; spoon <u>half</u> of meat layer over top. Sprinkle with <u>1 cup</u> Mozzarella cheese. Layer with remaining noodles. Spread with remaining filling; spoon remaining meat layer over top. Cover with aluminum foil; bake 40 minutes. Uncover; sprinkle with remaining Mozzarella cheese. Continue baking for 5 to 10 minutes or until heated through. Let stand 10 minutes before serving. **YIELD:** 12 servings.

* ³/₄ teaspoon <u>each</u> dried oregano leaves, dried marjoram leaves and dried basil leaves can be substituted for 1 tablespoon Italian herb seasoning.

** 1 (12-ounce) container cream-style cottage cheese, drained, can be substituted for 1 (15-ounce) container ricotta cheese.

*Nutrition Information (1 serving): Calories 320; Protein 24g; Carbohydrate 24g; Fat 14g;
Cholesterol 80mg; Sodium 760mg*

Curried Chicken & Vegetables

*The flavors of India are reflected in this pasta
made with a blend of spices.*

Preparation time: 30 minutes • Cooking time: 34 minutes

6 ounces (1 cup) uncooked
   dried rosamarina pasta
   (orzo)
3 tablespoons
   LAND O LAKES® Butter
2 medium (1 cup) onions,
   chopped
2 teaspoons grated fresh
   gingerroot
1 tablespoon curry powder
1 teaspoon coriander
1 teaspoon cumin
1 teaspoon turmeric
1 teaspoon cardamom
1 pound whole boneless
   chicken breasts, skinned,
   cut into 1-inch pieces
1 cup cauliflower flowerets
2 medium (1 cup) carrots,
   sliced 1/8-inch
1 (10 1/4-ounce) can chicken
   broth
1/2 cup frozen baby peas
1 tablespoon lime juice

Condiments
Major Grey chutney
Coarsely chopped peanuts <u>or</u>
   cashews
Raisins
Shredded coconut
Sliced bananas

Prepare pasta according to package directions. Drain. Set aside. Meanwhile, in 10-inch skillet melt butter until sizzling; add onions and gingerroot. Cook over medium heat, stirring occasionally, until onions are soft (5 to 8 minutes). Add curry, coriander, cumin, turmeric and cardamom. Continue cooking, stirring constantly, 30 seconds. Add chicken. Continue cooking, stirring constantly, until chicken is lightly browned (6 to 8 minutes). Add cauliflower, carrots and chicken broth. Cover; reduce heat to medium low. Continue cooking, stirring occasionally, until carrots and cauliflower are crisply tender (10 to 12 minutes). Stir in pasta, peas and lime juice. Continue cooking, stirring occasionally, until heated through (3 to 5 minutes). Serve with condiments. **YIELD:** 4 servings.

Nutrition Information (1 serving): Calories 430; Protein 34g; Carbohydrate 43g; Fat 13g; Cholesterol 90mg; Sodium 420mg.

Chicken & Vegetables *over* Fettuccine

*Serve with crusty
French bread.*

Preparation time: 20 minutes • Cooking time: 22 minutes

6 ounces uncooked dried
  fettuccine
1/4 cup LAND O LAKES®
  Butter
2 (12 ounces each) whole
  boneless chicken breasts,
  skinned, cut into 1/2-inch
  lengthwise strips
2 teaspoons finely chopped
  fresh garlic
2 cups (8 ounces) fresh
  mushrooms, cut into
  quarters
1 large onion, cut into rings
1 small green pepper, cut into
  strips
1 small red pepper, cut into
  strips
1 tablespoon all-purpose flour
1 cup whipping cream
1/4 cup dry white wine <u>or</u>
  chicken broth
1/2 teaspoon salt

Coarsely ground pepper
Freshly grated Parmesan
  cheese

Cook fettuccine according to package directions. Drain. Return to saucepan; set aside. Meanwhile, in 10-inch skillet melt butter until sizzling; add chicken and garlic. Cook over medium high heat, stirring constantly, 4 minutes. Stir in mushrooms, onion and pepper strips. Continue cooking, stirring constantly, until chicken is fork tender and vegetables are crisply tender (3 1/2 to 4 minutes). Using slotted spoon, remove chicken and vegetables; keep warm. In same skillet melt butter over medium heat; stir in flour until smooth and bubbly (1 minute). Add whipping cream, wine and salt; continue cooking, whisking constantly, until mixture comes to a full boil (6 to 8 minutes). Boil 1 minute. Add chicken and vegetables to cream mixture. Continue cooking, stirring constantly, until heated through (1 to 2 minutes). Pour mixture over hot cooked fettuccine; toss well to combine. Serve with pepper and Parmesan cheese.
YIELD: 6 servings.

Nutrition Information (1 serving): Calories 440; Protein 24g; Carbohydrate 29g; Fat 25g; Cholesterol 120mg; Sodium 320mg.

Angel Hair Pasta *with* Basil & Shrimp

**Basil accents shrimp and tomatoes
served over pasta.**

Preparation time: 20 minutes • Cooking time: 16 minutes

8 ounces uncooked dried
  angel hair pasta (very thin
  spaghetti) <u>or</u> vermicelli
1/4 cup olive <u>or</u> vegetable oil
1 teaspoon finely chopped
  fresh garlic
1 pound (40 to 45 medium)
  fresh <u>or</u> frozen raw shrimp,
  shelled, deveined, rinsed
1/4 cup chopped fresh parsley
1/2 cup dry white wine <u>or</u>
  chicken broth
2 (28-ounce) cans Italian <u>or</u>
  plum tomatoes, drained,
  cut up
3 tablespoons chopped fresh
  basil leaves*

Freshly grated Parmesan
  cheese

Cook pasta according to package directions. Drain. Toss with <u>1 tablespoon</u> oil. Keep warm. In 10-inch skillet heat remaining oil; add garlic. Cook over medium high heat, stirring constantly, until garlic is tender (30 to 60 seconds). Add shrimp; continue cooking, stirring constantly, until shrimp turn pink (1 to 2 minutes). Remove shrimp; set aside. Stir in all remaining ingredients <u>except</u> Parmesan cheese. Continue cooking, stirring occasionally, until liquid is reduced by half (7 to 10 minutes). Add shrimp; continue cooking until shrimp are heated through (2 to 3 minutes). Serve over hot cooked pasta; sprinkle with Parmesan cheese.
YIELD: 6 servings.

*2 teaspoons dried basil leaves can be substituted for 3 tablespoons chopped fresh basil leaves.

Nutrition Information (1 serving): Calories 300; Protein 10g; Carbohydrate 41g; Fat 10g; Cholesterol 28mg; Sodium 490mg.

Roasted Red Pepper & Scallop Fettuccine

*Roasted red pepper sauce adds color and flavor to
scallops served over pasta.*

Preparation time: 30 minutes • Baking time: 35 minutes • Cooking time: 14 minutes

2 whole red peppers

16 ounces uncooked dried
fettuccine

1/4 cup LAND O LAKES®
Butter

2 teaspoons finely chopped
fresh garlic

1/2 cup sliced green onions

1 1/2 pounds fresh or frozen
large scallops

2 cups LAND O LAKES®
Light Sour Cream

Salt

Coarsely ground pepper

Heat oven to 400°. Place whole red peppers on cookie sheet.
Bake, turning occasionally, for 25 to 35 minutes or until skins
are blackened. Cook; remove skins and seeds. In 5-cup blender
container puree peppers on High until smooth (30 to 45 seconds).
Set aside. Cook fettuccine according to package directions. Drain.
Meanwhile, in 10-inch skillet melt butter until sizzling; add
garlic. Cook over medium heat, stirring occasionally, 1 minute.
Add green onions and scallops. Continue cooking, stirring
occasionally, until scallops are tender (5 to 7 minutes). Stir in
sour cream and red pepper puree until well mixed. Continue
cooking until heated through (4 to 6 minutes). In large bowl toss
together scallop mixture and hot fettuccine. Season to taste.
YIELD: 8 servings.

*Nutrition Information (1 serving): Calories 400; Protein 24g; Carbohydrate 51g; Fat 11g;
Cholesterol 55mg; Sodium 240mg.*

Vegetable & Pasta Toss

Fresh garden vegetables bring a homemade taste
to this unique dish.

Preparation time: 25 minutes • Cooking time: 4 minutes

6 ounces uncooked dried
linguine

2 medium (2 cups) zucchini,
sliced 1/4-inch

2 medium (2 cups) summer
squash, sliced 1/4-inch

1/4 cup LAND O LAKES®
Butter

2 teaspoons chopped fresh
dill weed*

1/4 teaspoon salt

1/8 teaspoon pepper

1 teaspoon lemon juice

1/2 pint cherry tomatoes,
halved

Freshly grated Parmesan
cheese

Cook linguine according to package directions. Drain. Meanwhile, in 10-inch skillet bring 1/2 inch water to a full boil; add zucchini and summer squash. Cover; cook over medium high heat until vegetables are crisply tender (3 to 4 minutes). Drain; set aside. In same pan used to prepare linguine, melt butter until sizzling; stir in dill, salt, pepper and lemon juice. Remove from heat. Add linguine, cooked vegetables and tomatoes; toss lightly to coat. Serve with Parmesan cheese. **YIELD:** 6 servings.

*2 teaspoons dried dill weed can be substituted for 2 tablespoons fresh dill.

Nutrition Information (1 serving): Calories 190; Protein 5g; Carbohydrate 24g; Fat 8g;
Cholesterol 20mg; Sodium 170mg.

Spinach Stuffed Pasta Shells

These pasta shells, stuffed with a unique vegetable mixture, make an interesting main dish accompaniment.

Preparation time: 20 minutes • Cooking time: 7 minutes • Baking time: 16 minutes

12 uncooked dried jumbo
   pasta shells

1/4 cup LAND O LAKES®
   Butter

2 tablespoons pine nuts <u>or</u>
   sliced almonds

7 ounces fresh spinach, torn

1 cup sliced 1/4-inch fresh
   mushrooms

1/2 teaspoon fennel seed

1/2 teaspoon finely chopped
   fresh garlic

1/2 cup crushed croutons <u>or</u>
   dried crumbly style herb
   seasoned stuffing

1/2 cup (2 ounces)
   LAND O LAKES®
   Cheddar Cheese, shredded

1 tablespoon
   LAND O LAKES® Butter,
   melted

Freshly grated Parmesan
   cheese

Paprika

Heat oven to 375°. Prepare pasta shells according to package directions. Drain. Set aside. In 10-inch skillet melt 1/4 cup butter until sizzling; add pine nuts. Cook over medium heat until toasted (2 to 4 minutes). Add spinach, mushrooms, fennel and garlic; continue cooking until spinach is wilted (2 to 3 minutes). Stir in croutons and Cheddar cheese. Fill each cooked pasta shell with about <u>2 tablespoons</u> spinach mixture. Place in 9-inch square baking pan. Brush with 1 tablespoon melted butter. Sprinkle with Parmesan cheese and paprika. Cover with aluminum foil; bake 12 minutes. Uncover; continue baking for 2 to 4 minutes or until lightly browned. **YIELD:** 4 servings.

Nutrition Information (1 serving): Calories 470; Protein 15g; Carbohydrate 49g; Fat 24g; Cholesterol 55mg; Sodium 480mg.

Pasta *with* Artichoke Hearts

A rich, tangy pasta sauce with artichoke hearts and red pepper.

Preparation time: 20 minutes • Cooking time: 13 minutes

8 ounces uncooked dried
   spinach fettuccine
1 cup mayonnaise
1 1/2 cups milk
1 tablespoon all-purpose flour
1 cup (4 ounces)
   LAND O LAKES®
   Mozzarella Cheese,
   shredded
1/2 cup chopped fresh parsley
1/4 cup freshly grated
   Parmesan cheese
1 medium (1 cup) red pepper,
   coarsely chopped
1 (14-ounce) can artichoke
   hearts, drained, quartered
1/2 teaspoon coarsely ground
   pepper
1/8 teaspoon ground red
   pepper
1 teaspoon finely chopped
   fresh garlic

Cook fettuccine according to package directions. Drain. Meanwhile, in 10-inch skillet, with wire whisk, stir together mayonnaise, milk and flour. Cook over medium heat, stirring occasionally, until smooth (2 to 3 minutes). Add all remaining ingredients <u>except</u> fettuccine. Continue cooking, stirring occasionally, until mixture comes to a full boil (6 to 10 minutes). Serve over hot cooked fettuccine. **YIELD:** 6 servings.

Nutrition Information (1 serving): Calories 540; Protein 16g; Carbohydrate 40g; Fat 36g; Cholesterol 40mg; Sodium 450mg.

Fettuccine *with* Asparagus

*Crisply tender asparagus and fettuccine are complemented
with fresh rosemary.*

Preparation time: 20 minutes • Cooking time: 14 minutes

2 ounces uncooked dried
  fettuccine

2 tablespoons olive <u>or</u>
  vegetable oil

1/4 cup chopped onion

2 teaspoons finely chopped
  fresh garlic

3/4 pound (18) fresh
  asparagus spears, trimmed,
  cut into thirds*

1/2 teaspoon chopped fresh
  rosemary leaves**

1/8 teaspoon salt

1/8 teaspoon pepper

1/2 cup half-and-half

1/3 cup freshly grated Romano
  <u>or</u> Parmesan cheese

Cook fettuccine according to package directions. Drain. Meanwhile, in 10-inch skillet heat oil; stir in onion and garlic. Cook over medium heat, stirring occasionally, until onion is crisply tender (2 to 3 minutes). Stir in asparagus, rosemary, salt and pepper. Continue cooking, stirring occasionally, until asparagus turns bright green (2 to 3 minutes); cover. Continue cooking, stirring occasionally, until asparagus is crisply tender (5 to 6 minutes). Stir in fettuccine, half-and-half and cheese. Continue cooking, stirring constantly, until heated through (1 to 2 minutes). Serve immediately.
YIELD: 6 servings.

*1 (9 ounce) package frozen asparagus cuts can be substituted for 3/4 pound (18) fresh asparagus spears, trimmed, cut into thirds.

**1/8 teaspoon crushed dried rosemary leaves can be substituted for 1/2 teaspoon chopped fresh rosemary leaves.

*Nutrition Information (1 serving): Calories 140; Protein 6g; Carbohydrate 11g; Fat 9g;
Cholesterol 15mg; Sodium 130mg.*

Country Vegetable Lasagna

*You won't miss the meat in this flavorful
cheese lasagna.*

Preparation time: 45 minutes • Cooking time: 42 minutes • Baking time: 35 minutes

Pasta

9 uncooked dried lasagna
   noodles

Sauce

3 tablespoons olive <u>or</u>
   vegetable oil

2 cups (8 ounces) coarsely
   chopped fresh mushrooms

1 medium (1 cup) green
   pepper, chopped

1 medium (1/2 cup) onion,
   chopped

1 teaspoon finely chopped
   fresh garlic

1/4 cup chopped fresh parsley

1 (28-ounce) can whole
   tomatoes, undrained, cut up

1 (12-ounce) can tomato paste

2 teaspoons sugar

1 teaspoon dried basil leaves

1 teaspoon dried oregano
   leaves

2 bay leaves

Cheese Mixture

1/4 cup freshly grated
   Parmesan cheese

1 (15-ounce) carton ricotta
   cheese*

2 eggs

1/4 teaspoon pepper

3 cups (12 ounces)
   LAND O LAKES®
   Mozzarella Cheese,
   shredded

1/4 cup freshly grated
   Parmesan cheese

Cook lasagna noodles according to package directions. Drain. Meanwhile, in 10-inch skillet heat oil; add mushrooms, green pepper, onion and garlic. Cook over medium heat, stirring occasionally, until vegetables are crisply tender (7 to 9 minutes). Stir in all remaining sauce ingredients. Continue cooking, stirring occasionally, until mixture comes to a full boil (2 to 3 minutes). Reduce heat to low; continue cooking, stirring occasionally, 30 minutes. Remove bay leaves. Meanwhile, in medium bowl stir together 1/4 cup Parmesan cheese, ricotta cheese, eggs and pepper. <u>Heat oven to 350°.</u> On bottom of 13x9-inch baking pan spread <u>1 cup</u> sauce. Top with <u>3</u> lasagna noodles, <u>1/3</u> cheese mixture, <u>1/3</u> sauce and <u>1 cup</u> Mozzarella cheese. Repeat layers 2 more times, ending with Mozzarella cheese. Sprinkle with 1/4 cup Parmesan cheese. Bake for 30 to 35 minutes or until bubbly and heated through. Let stand 10 minutes.
YIELD: 8 servings.

*2 cups cottage cheese can be substituted for 1 (15 ounce) carton ricotta cheese.

*Nutrition Information (1 serving): Calories 460; Protein 29g; Carbohydrate 40g; Fat 21g;
Cholesterol 110mg; Sodium 1010mg.*

Vegetable Medley *with* Pasta

Ziti pasta comes shaped in long,
thin tubes.

Preparation time: 15 minutes • Cooking time: 6 minutes

4 ounces (1 1/4 cups)
  uncooked dried ziti pasta
2 tablespoons olive or
  vegetable oil
2 teaspoons finely chopped
  fresh garlic
1 (16-ounce) package frozen
  vegetable mixture (broccoli,
  red pepper, cauliflower,
  pearl onions, carrots, etc.)
1/4 cup white wine or
  chicken broth
1/2 cup freshly grated
  Parmesan cheese
1/4 cup chopped fresh basil
  leaves*
1/8 teaspoon salt
1/8 teaspoon pepper

Cook pasta according to package directions. Drain. Meanwhile, in 10-inch skillet heat oil; add garlic. Stir in vegetable mixture. Cook over medium high heat, stirring constantly, 1 minute. Reduce heat to medium. Stir in wine. Cover; continue cooking, stirring occasionally, until vegetables are crisply tender (3 to 5 minutes). Place pasta in large bowl; toss with vegetables and all remaining ingredients. **YIELD:** 6 servings.

*1 tablespoon dried basil leaves can be substituted for 1/4 cup chopped fresh basil leaves.

Nutrition Information (1 serving): Calories 180; Protein 9g; Carbohydrate 25g; Fat 5g; Cholesterol 5mg; Sodium 240mg.

Pasta with Fresh Tomatoes

This pleasing recipe combines ripe Roma tomatoes,
fresh herbs and a unique pasta.

Preparation time: 25 minutes • Cooking time: 6 minutes (also pictured on cover)

4 ounces (1 1/2 cups)
　uncooked dried mini lasagna
　noodles or bow tie pasta
2 tablespoons
　LAND O LAKES® Butter
4 medium (2 cups) ripe Roma
　tomatoes, seeded, cut into
　1-inch pieces*
2 tablespoons chopped fresh
　basil leaves**
1 tablespoon chopped fresh
　oregano leaves***
1/8 teaspoon salt
1/8 teaspoon pepper
2 teaspoons finely chopped
　fresh garlic
1/3 cup freshly grated
　Parmesan cheese

Cook noodles according to package directions. Drain. Meanwhile, in 10-inch skillet melt butter until sizzling; stir in tomatoes, basil, oregano, salt, pepper and garlic. Cook over medium high heat, stirring constantly, until heated through (2 to 3 minutes). Add noodles. Continue cooking, stirring occasionally, until flavors are blended (2 to 3 minutes). Toss with Parmesan cheese. Serve immediately. **YIELD:** 6 servings.

*2 medium (2 cups) ripe tomatoes, seeded, cut into 1-inch pieces, can be substituted for 4 medium (2 cups) ripe Roma tomatoes, seeded, cut into 1-inch pieces.

**2 teaspoons dried basil leaves can be substituted for 2 tablespoons chopped fresh basil leaves.

***1 teaspoon dried oregano leaves can be substituted for 1 tablespoon chopped fresh oregano leaves.

Nutrition Information (1 serving): Calories 140; Protein 5g; Carbohydrate 17g; Fat 6g; Cholesterol 15mg; Sodium 190mg.

Skillet Pasta & Vegetables

*A new way to use the plentiful zucchini
from your garden.*

Preparation time: 20 minutes • Cooking time: 9 minutes

4 ounces (1 1/2 cups)
uncooked dried bow tie
pasta*

1/4 cup LAND O LAKES®
Butter

1 teaspoon finely chopped
fresh garlic

1 medium zucchini, cut into
1/2-inch pieces

1 small eggplant, cut into
1/2-inch pieces

1 medium red onion, cut into
eighths

1 teaspoon dried basil leaves

1/2 teaspoon salt

1/2 teaspoon pepper

1 1/2 cups (6 ounces)
LAND O LAKES®
Mozzarella Cheese,
shredded

Cook pasta according to package directions. Drain. In 10-inch skillet melt butter until sizzling; stir in garlic. Stir in all remaining ingredients <u>except</u> pasta and cheese. Cook over medium heat, stirring occasionally, until vegetables are crisply tender (4 to 6 minutes). Stir in pasta. Continue cooking, stirring occasionally, until heated through (2 to 3 minutes). Stir in cheese. Serve immediately. **YIELD:** 4 servings.

*4 ounces (2 cups) your favorite uncooked dried pasta can be substituted for 4 ounces (2 cups) uncooked dried bow tie pasta.

Nutrition Information (1 serving): Calories 350; Protein 17g; Carbohydrate 29g; Fat 20g; Cholesterol 55mg; Sodium 610mg.

Quick Tortellini Supper

Fresh pasta combines with mushrooms, peas and cheese for an easy meal.

Preparation time: 15 minutes • Cooking time: 10 minutes

18 ounces (4 cups) fresh
   tortellini*
1/4 cup LAND O LAKES®
   Butter
1 cup sliced fresh mushrooms
1 (10-ounce) package frozen
   peas, thawed
1 1/2 cups (6 ounces)
   LAND O LAKES®
   Cheddar Cheese, shredded
Salt and pepper

Cook tortellini according to package directions. Drain. Set aside. In 10-inch skillet melt butter until sizzling; add mushrooms. Cook over medium heat, stirring occasionally, until tender (3 to 5 minutes). Stir in tortellini and peas; continue cooking until heated through (3 to 5 minutes). Stir in 1 cup cheese; salt and pepper to taste. Sprinkle with remaining cheese. **YIELD:** 4 servings.

*7 ounces (1 1/2 cups) uncooked dried tortellini or 8 ounces (2 1/2 cups) uncooked dried medium macaroni shells can be substituted for 18 ounces (4 cups) fresh tortellini. Cook according to package directions; drain.

Nutrition Information (1 serving): Calories 650; Protein 34g; Carbohydrate 47g; Fat 36g; Cholesterol 230mg; Sodium 940mg.

Pasta Primavera

*A variety of colorful, flavorful vegetables
simmer in a white wine sauce.*

Preparation time: 30 minutes • Cooking time: 19 minutes

1 (9-ounce) package
    uncooked fresh linguine*

3 tablespoons olive <u>or</u>
    vegetable oil

1 medium red onion,
    thinly sliced

1/2 teaspoon finely chopped
    fresh garlic

2 medium (2 cups) yellow
    summer squash, halved
    lengthwise, sliced 1/8-inch

1 medium (1 cup) ripe
    tomato, cubed 1/2-inch

1 medium red <u>or</u> green pepper,
    cut into 1/4-inch strips

1 pound (24) asparagus spears,
    trimmed, cut into thirds

1/2 cup dry white wine <u>or</u>
    chicken broth

2 tablespoons chopped fresh
    dill**

1/4 teaspoon salt

1/4 teaspoon coarsely ground
    pepper

1/4 cup freshly grated
    Parmesan cheese

Freshly grated Parmesan
    cheese

Cook linguine according to package directions. Drain. Meanwhile, in 10-inch skillet heat oil; add onion and garlic. Cook over medium heat, stirring occasionally, until onion is crisply tender (3 to 4 minutes). Add squash, tomato, red pepper and asparagus. Continue cooking, stirring occasionally, until vegetables are crisply tender (8 to 10 minutes). Stir in wine, dill weed, salt and pepper. Continue cooking, stirring occasionally, until heated through (4 to 5 minutes). Serve over hot cooked linguine with 1/4 cup Parmesan cheese. Serve with additional Parmesan cheese. **YIELD:** 6 servings.

* 9 ounces uncooked dried linguine can be substituted for 1 (9 ounce) package uncooked fresh linguine.

** 2 teaspoons dried dill weed can be substituted for 2 tablespoons chopped fresh dill.

Nutrition Information (1 serving): Calories 290; Protein 11g; Carbohydrates 41g; Fat 9g; Cholesterol 2mg; Sodium 180mg.

Vegetable & Pasta Pesto Soup

*Use homemade or purchased pesto to stir into this
vegetable soup for extra flavor.*

Preparation time: 45 minutes • Cooking time: 43 minutes

3 tablespoons olive <u>or</u>
  vegetable oil
1/2 cup sliced 1/8-inch leeks
2 medium (1 cup) onions,
  chopped
5 (14 1/2-ounce) cans low
  sodium chicken broth
2 medium (1 cup) carrots,
  sliced 1/8-inch
2 stalks (1 cup) celery, sliced
  1/8-inch
1 tablespoon chopped fresh
  thyme leaves*
1/4 pound (1 cup) fresh green
  beans, cut into thirds
2 cups fresh spinach, torn
  into bite-size pieces**
1 medium (1 cup) ripe tomato,
  peeled, seeded, cut into
  1/2-inch pieces
1 medium (1 cup) zucchini, cut
  in half lengthwise, then
  into 1/2-inch slices
1 (15-ounce) can cannellini
  beans, rinsed, drained
1/2 teaspoon salt
1/4 teaspoon pepper
7 ounces (1 1/2 cups)
  uncooked dried pasta rings

1/2 cup pesto sauce
Freshly grated Parmesan
  cheese

In Dutch oven heat oil; add leeks and onions. Cook over medium
heat, stirring occasionally, until onions are soft (5 to 8 minutes).
Add chicken broth, carrots, celery and thyme. Cook over high
heat until soup just comes to a boil (4 to 5 minutes). Cover; reduce
heat to medium. Continue cooking until carrots are crisply tender
(13 to 15 minutes). Add green beans; continue cooking 4 minutes.
Stir in spinach, tomato, zucchini, cannellini beans, salt and pepper.
Continue cooking, stirring occasionally, 5 minutes. Add pasta.
Continue cooking, stirring occasionally, until pasta is tender
(5 to 6 minutes). To serve, ladle soup into bowls. Spoon
1 tablespoon pesto sauce into each bowl; sprinkle with
Parmesan cheese. **YIELD:** 8 servings.

* 1 teaspoon dried thyme leaves can be substituted for 1 tablespoon chopped fresh
thyme leaves.

** 1 (10 ounce) package frozen chopped spinach, thawed, can be substituted for
2 cups fresh spinach, torn into bite-size pieces.

*Nutrition Information (1 serving): Calories 320; Protein 12g; Carbohydrate 35g; Fat 15g;
Cholesterol 0mg; Sodium 270mg.*

Black Bean Chicken Salad

Serve this substantial main dish salad with thick slices
of warm-from-the-oven sourdough bread.

Preparation time: 30 minutes • Chilling time: 4 hours

4 ounces (1 cup) uncooked
dried cavatelli pasta <u>or</u>
medium pasta shells

Dressing

$^1/_3$ cup olive <u>or</u> vegetable oil

$^1/_3$ cup lemon juice

1 teaspoon sugar

$^1/_2$ teaspoon pepper

2 tablespoons chopped fresh
basil leaves*

2 tablespoons chopped fresh
parsley

3 tablespoons water

$^1/_2$ teaspoon hot pepper sauce

Salad

$1^1/_2$ cups cubed 1-inch cooked
chicken

1 cup (4 ounces)
LAND O LAKES® Cheddar
Cheese, cubed

1 medium (1 cup) yellow
summer squash, cut into
$^1/_4$-inch slices, halved

1 small red <u>or</u> green pepper,
cut into $^1/_4$-inch strips,
halved crosswise

1 (15-ounce) can black beans,
rinsed, drained

Lettuce leaves

Cook pasta according to package directions. Rinse with cold water; drain. Meanwhile, in jar with tight-fitting lid combine all dressing ingredients; shake well. In large bowl combine pasta and all salad ingredients <u>except</u> lettuce leaves. Shake dressing well; pour over pasta mixture. Toss lightly to coat. Cover; refrigerate 4 hours or overnight. Line 4 plates with lettuce leaves; top with pasta mixture.

YIELD: 4 servings.

*2 teaspoons dried basil leaves can be substituted for 2 tablespoons chopped
fresh basil leaves.

Nutrition Information (1 serving): Calories 580; Protein 32g; Carbohydrate 41g; Fat 32g;
Cholesterol 75mg; Sodium 230mg

Fettuccine Chicken Salad

*A colorful mix of fresh vegetables, chicken and fettuccine
makes this a hearty main dish salad.*

Preparation time: 45 minutes

Dressing

2/3 cup vegetable oil

1/2 cup white wine vinegar

1 teaspoon dried basil leaves

1 teaspoon dried oregano
  leaves

1 teaspoon finely chopped
  fresh garlic

1 teaspoon salt

1/2 teaspoon pepper

Salad

6 ounces uncooked dried
  fettuccine, broken into thirds

2 1/2 cups cubed 1-inch cooked
  chicken <u>or</u> turkey

2 cups broccoli flowerets

2 medium (1 cup) carrots,
  sliced 1/4-inch

1/2 medium red onion, sliced
  into 1/8-inch rings

1 cup cherry tomatoes, halved

In jar with tight-fitting lid combine all dressing ingredients; shake well. Set aside. Cook fettuccine according to package directions. Rinse with cold water; drain. In large bowl combine fettuccine and all remaining salad ingredients. Gently stir in dressing. **YIELD:** 6 servings.

Nutrition Information (1 serving): Calories 450; Protein 22g; Carbohydrate 27g; Fat 29g; Cholesterol 50mg; Sodium 420mg.

Peppery Pasta Salad

*This one-bowl salad gets a burst of flavor
from jalapeno cheese.*

Preparation time: 30 minutes • Chilling time: 2 hours

4 ounces (2 cups) uncooked
   dried rotini (corkscrew <u>or</u>
   pasta twists)

1 slice (1/2-inch thick)
   cooked turkey <u>or</u> ham (8 to
   10 ounces), cubed 1/2-inch

6 ounces LAND O LAKES®
   Jalapeño Cheese Food,
   cubed 1/2-inch

12 cherry tomatoes, halved

1/2 medium green pepper, cut
   into strips

1/2 medium red pepper, cut
   into strips

2/3 cup creamy Italian
   dressing

Cook rotini according to package directions. Rinse with cold
water; drain. In large bowl combine rotini and all remaining
ingredients until well coated. Cover; refrigerate at least 2 hours.
YIELD: 6 servings.

*Nutrition Information (1 serving): Calories 330; Protein 19g; Carbohydrate 19g; Fat 18g;
Cholesterol 50mg; Sodium 620mg.*

Dill 'N Salmon Pasta Salad

*A light, refreshing summertime supper. Serve this pasta salad
with multi-grain bread and fresh fruit.*

Preparation time: 30 minutes • Chilling time: 1 hour

7 ounces (2 1/4 cups)
  uncooked dried rotini
  (corkscrew <u>or</u> pasta twists)
1/3 cup cubed 1/2-inch red
  pepper
1/3 cup vegetable oil
1/4 cup lemon juice
8 ounces salmon fillet, cooked,
  chunked
8 ounces (2 cups)
  LAND O LAKES® Cheddar
  Cheese, cubed 1/2-inch
1 teaspoon dried dill weed
1/2 teaspoon garlic salt
2 tablespoons sliced green
  onions
Salt and pepper

Cook rotini according to package directions. Rinse with cold water;
drain. In large bowl gently stir together all ingredients; season with
salt and pepper to taste. Cover; refrigerate at least 1 hour.
YIELD: 6 servings.

TIP: To cook salmon, place in 10-inch skillet; cover with water. Cook over
medium heat until salmon flakes with a fork (12 to 15 minutes).

*Nutrition Information (1 serving): Calories 440; Protein 21g; Carbohydrate 25g; Fat 28g;
Cholesterol 60mg; Sodium 410mg.*

Crab & Pasta Salad

This delightful salad makes enough to serve a crowd.

Preparation time: 30 minutes • Chilling time: 2 hours

Salad

1 (16-ounce) package
   uncooked dried rosamarina
   pasta (orzo)*

2 cups small broccoli flowerets

4 medium (2 cups) carrots,
   thinly sliced

2 stalks (1 cup) celery,
   coarsely chopped

3/4 cup chopped red onion

2 (8-ounce) packages
   imitation crab legs
   (surimi), cut into 1/2-inch
   pieces

Dressing

2 cups LAND O LAKES®
   Light Sour Cream

2 (8-ounce) cartons (2 cups)
   lowfat plain yogurt

2 to 3 tablespoons chopped
   fresh thyme leaves**

1 teaspoon salt

1/2 teaspoon pepper

Cook pasta according to package directions. Rinse pasta with cold water; drain. In very large bowl combine pasta and all remaining salad ingredients. In medium bowl stir together all dressing ingredients. Gently stir dressing into salad. Cover; refrigerate at least 2 hours. **YIELD:** 16 servings.

* 2 (7 ounce) packages uncooked dried pasta rings can be substituted for 1 (16 ounce) package uncooked dried rosamarina pasta (orzo).

** 2 teaspoons dried thyme leaves can be substituted for 2 to 3 tablespoons chopped fresh thyme leaves.

Nutrition Information (1 serving); Calories 190; Protein 11g; Carbohydrate 31g; Fat 3g; Cholesterol 15mg; Sodium 230mg.

Sunshine Pasta Salad

*Prepare this lemon pasta salad when tomatoes are
garden-ripe and bursting with flavor.*

Preparation time: 30 minutes

4 ounces (1 1/4 cups)
    uncooked dried rotini
    (corkscrew <u>or</u> pasta twists)
1 (6-ounce) jar marinated
    artichoke hearts, quartered,
    <u>reserve marinade</u>
1/2 cup chopped fresh parsley
1 medium (1 cup) cucumber,
    sliced 1/8-inch
1/2 teaspoon salt
1/2 teaspoon dried dill weed
1/4 teaspoon pepper
1 tablespoon grated lemon peel
2 tablespoons lemon juice
4 medium ripe tomatoes

Cook rotini according to package directions. Rinse with cold water; drain. In large bowl combine rotini, artichokes, reserved marinade and all remaining ingredients <u>except</u> tomatoes. Remove stems from tomatoes; cut <u>each</u> tomato into 4 wedges, leaving 1/2-inch base to keep tomato intact. Serve <u>1 cup</u> pasta over each tomato. **YIELD:** 4 servings.

Nutrition Information (1 serving): Calories220; Protein 6g; Carbohydrate 33g; Fat 8g; Cholestrol 0mg; Sodium 430mg.

Pasta *with* Mixed Salad Greens & Raspberries

Crisp salad greens and pasta are served with a light vinaigrette dressing.

Preparation time: 30 minutes

2 ounces (1/2 cup) uncooked dried cavatelli pasta <u>or</u> medium pasta shells

Dressing
1/3 cup olive <u>or</u> vegetable oil
1/4 cup raspberry vinegar <u>or</u> white wine vinegar
1/4 teaspoon finely chopped fresh garlic
1/8 teaspoon salt
1/8 teaspoon coarsely ground pepper

Salad
3 cups mixed salad greens (romaine lettuce, Bibb lettuce, curly endive, radicchio, red cabbage, etc.)
1/2 cup fresh <u>or</u> frozen no sugar added raspberries
1 tablespoon chopped fresh mint leaves

Cook pasta according to package directions. Rinse with cold water; drain. Meanwhile, in jar with tight fitting lid combine all dressing ingredients; shake well. Just before serving, in large bowl combine pasta and all salad ingredients. Gently stir in <u>1/4 cup</u> dressing. Serve remaining dressing with salad. **YIELD:** 6 servings.

TIP: Mixed or fancy mixed salad greens can be found in your grocer's produce section.

Nutrition Information (1 serving): Calories 150; Protein 2g; Carbohydrate 9g; Fat 12g; Cholesterol 0mg; Sodium 50mg.

Terrific Chicken!

Cashew-Top Sesame Chicken and
Provolone-Chicken Individual Pizzas

Cashew-Top Sesame Chicken

*Sesame seed, cashews and herbs garnish baked chicken
for a crispy golden main dish.*

Preparation time: 15 minutes • Baking time: 1 hour 18 minutes (pictured on page 78)

³/4 **cup dried bread crumbs**

2 **tablespoons sesame seed**

¹/2 **teaspoon onion salt**

¹/2 **teaspoon dried basil leaves**

¹/2 **teaspoon dried rosemary,
crushed**

¹/4 **teaspoon garlic powder**

¹/4 **teaspoon paprika**

¹/8 **teaspoon pepper**

1 **(3 to 4-pound) frying
chicken, cut into 8 pieces**

²/3 **cup LAND O LAKES®
Butter, melted**

¹/4 **cup chopped salted cashews
or peanuts**

Heat oven to 375°. In 9-inch pie pan combine all ingredients <u>except</u> chicken, butter and cashews. Dip chicken in <u>1/2 cup</u> melted butter, then roll in crumb mixture to coat. Place chicken, skin-side up, in 13x9-inch baking pan. Bake for 60 to 75 minutes or until chicken is fork tender. Meanwhile, stir cashews into remaining melted butter. When chicken is tender, pour cashew mixture over chicken. Continue baking for 3 minutes. **YIELD:** 6 servings.

*Nutrition Information (1 serving): Calories 610; Protein 18g; Carbohydrate 12g; Fat 55g;
Cholesterol 120mg; Sodium 530mg*

Provolone-Chicken Individual Pizzas

The highly seasoned pesto comes shining through while the olives and capers lend a slightly tangy flavor to this sophisticated pizza.

Preparation time: 20 minutes • Baking time: 15 minutes (pictured on page 79)

Crust
4 (6-inch) individual Italian
   bread shells <u>or</u> focaccia

Toppings
1/4 cup pesto
1 1/2 cups chopped cooked
   chicken
1/3 cup finely chopped red or
   white onion
1/4 cup sliced ripe olives
1 large (1 1/2 cups) ripe
   tomato, cubed 1/2 inch
1 tablespoon capers, drained,
   rinsed
4 (1 ounce each) slices
   LAND O LAKES®
   Provolone Cheese,
   cut into quarters*

Heat oven to 425°. Spread each flatbread round with <u>1 tablespoon</u> pesto. Place on cookie sheet. Arrange chicken, onion, olives, tomato and capers over rounds. Lay cheese quarters on top. Bake for 12 to 15 minutes or until heated through. **YIELD:** 4 servings.

* 1 cup (4 ounces) LAND O LAKES® Shredded Mozzarella Cheese can be substituted for 4 (1 ounce each) slices LAND O LAKES® Provolone Cheese, cut into quarters.

Nutrition Information (1 serving): Calories 640; Protein 39g; Carbohydrate 60g; Fat 30g; Cholesterol 80mg; Sodium 1130mg

Chicken Almondine Pastry

This sophisticated dinner-in-a-dish is lined with a buttery pastry and layered with savory chicken filling, crunchy almonds and deep green spinach.

Preparation time: 45 minutes • Chilling time: 1 hour • Cooking time: 9 minutes • Baking time: 25 minutes

Crust

1½ cups all-purpose flour

½ cup LAND O LAKES® Butter

1 egg, beaten

3 tablespoons milk

Sauce

½ cup LAND O LAKES® Butter

2 (8-ounce) packages (4 cups) fresh mushrooms, sliced ⅛-inch

1 pound boneless chicken breasts, skinned, cubed ½-inch

½ cup water

3 tablespoons cornstarch

1 teaspoon dried basil leaves

1 teaspoon instant chicken bouillon granules

¼ teaspoon garlic powder

¼ teaspoon pepper

Filling

½ cup sliced almonds

1 (10-ounce) package frozen chopped spinach, thawed, well drained

1 teaspoon sesame seed

Heat oven to 400°. In medium bowl place flour; cut in ½ cup butter until mixture is crumbly. In small bowl beat together egg and milk; reserve 1 teaspoon for crust. Add remaining egg mixture to flour mixture; stir until mixture leaves side of bowl and forms a ball. Divide dough into 2 balls; wrap balls in plastic food wrap. Refrigerate for 30 to 60 minutes. On lightly floured surface roll 1 ball into 12-inch round. Place in 9-inch pie pan. Trim edge even with pan; set aside. On lightly floured surface roll remaining ball into 11-inch round; set aside. In 10-inch skillet melt ½ cup butter until sizzling; stir in mushrooms and chicken. Cover; cook over medium heat, stirring occasionally, until chicken is fork tender (6 to 8 minutes). Meanwhile, in small bowl stir together all remaining sauce ingredients; stir into cooked chicken mixture. Continue cooking, stirring constantly, until mixture is bubbly and sauce turns translucent (30 to 60 seconds). Sprinkle almonds on bottom crust in pan; pour chicken mixture over almonds. Spread spinach over chicken mixture. Place top crust over spinach; tuck extra top crust under edges of bottom crust. Crimp or flute crust. Cut 8 slits in top crust; brush top crust (do not brush crimped edges) with reserved egg mixture. Sprinkle with sesame seed. Bake for 20 to 25 minutes or until golden brown. **YIELD:** 6 servings.

Nutrition Information (1 serving): Calories 580; Protein 26g; Carbohydrate 36g; Fat 39g; Cholesterol 160mg; Sodium 470mg

Stir-Fried Basil Chicken

Mushrooms and green onions are stir-fried then topped with fresh sweet basil leaves in this fragrant poultry dish.

Preparation time: 20 minutes • Standing time: 30 minutes • Cooking time: 9 minutes

Basil
2/3 cup packed (about 40) fresh basil leaves

Sauce
1/2 cup water
3 tablespoons soy sauce
3 tablespoons dry sherry <u>or</u> water
4 teaspoons cornstarch
1 teaspoon instant chicken bouillon granules

Vegetables
3 to 4 tablespoons vegetable oil
2 teaspoons finely chopped fresh garlic
12 (1½ cups) green onions, cut into 1-inch diagonal slices
2 (8-ounce) packages (4 cups) fresh mushrooms, sliced

Chicken
2 (12 ounces each) whole boneless chicken breasts, skinned, cut into 1-inch cubes

2 cups hot cooked rice

Wash basil leaves. Lay leaves in single layer on paper towels; pat dry. Let stand at room temperature for 30 minutes; pat leaves again with paper towels. In small bowl stir together all sauce ingredients; set aside. In wok or 10-inch skillet heat oil; add basil leaves. (Add more oil as needed during stir-frying.) Cook over medium high heat, stirring constantly, until glossy green (10 to 12 seconds). Use slotted spoon to remove basil leaves from hot oil; drain on paper towels. Add garlic to hot oil; cook over medium high heat, stirring constantly, 15 seconds. Add green onions; continue cooking, stirring constantly, 1 minute. Add mushrooms; continue cooking, stirring constantly, 1 minute. Remove vegetables from wok; set aside. Place chicken in hot wok; cook over medium high heat, stirring constantly, until chicken is fork tender (3 to 5 minutes). Push chicken from center of wok. Stir sauce; add sauce to center of wok. Cook, stirring constantly, until slightly thickened (1 to 2 minutes). Return cooked vegetables to wok; stir to coat with sauce. Cook, stirring constantly, until heated through (1 minute). Place on serving plate; sprinkle with cooked basil leaves. Serve over rice.
YIELD: 4 servings.

Nutrition Information (1 serving): Calories 500; Protein 43g; Carbohydrate 43g; Fat 15g; Cholesterol 100mg; Sodium 970mg

Curry-Garlic Chicken Stir-Fry

*A curry-soy flavored sauce rounds out the mellow
flavors of garlic and onion in this Thai-inspired stir-fry.*

Preparation time: 30 minutes • Cooking time: 11 minutes

Sauce

1/2	cup chicken broth
2	tablespoons soy sauce
2	tablespoons dry white wine <u>or</u> chicken broth
1	tablespoon cornstarch
2	teaspoons curry powder
1/2	teaspoon sugar

Vegetables

1 to 2	tablespoons vegetable oil
1	tablespoon finely chopped fresh garlic
1	large onion, cut into thin wedges
1	large (1 cup) green pepper, cut into 1-inch pieces
1	large (1 cup) red pepper, cut into 1-inch pieces
1	(8-ounce) can sliced bamboo shoots, drained

Chicken

2	(12 ounces each) whole boneless chicken breasts, skinned, cut into 1/2-inch strips
2	cups hot cooked rice

In small bowl combine all sauce ingredients; set aside. In wok or 10-inch skillet heat oil; add garlic. (Add more oil as needed during stir-frying.) Cook over medium high heat, stirring constantly, 15 seconds. Add onion; continue cooking, stirring constantly, 1 minute. Add green and red peppers; continue cooking, stirring constantly, 1 minute. Add bamboo shoots; continue cooking, stirring constantly, until vegetables are crisply tender (1 minute). Remove vegetables from wok; set aside. Place chicken in hot wok; cook over medium high heat, stirring constantly, until chicken is fork tender (3 to 5 minutes). Push chicken from center of wok. Stir sauce; add sauce to center of wok. Cook, stirring constantly, until slightly thickened (1 to 2 minutes). Return cooked vegetables to wok; stir to coat with sauce. Cook, stirring constantly, until heated through (1 minute). Serve over rice.
YIELD: 4 servings.

Nutrition Information (1 serving): Calories 430; Protein 42g; Carbohydrate 42g; Fat 9g; Cholesterol 100mg; Sodium 710mg

Fruited-Ginger Chicken Stir-Fry

*As you eat this delightful fresh fruit stir-fry, you experience
the crunch of apples and the tart sweetness of oranges.*

Preparation time: 40 minutes • Cooking time: 8 minutes

Sauce
3/4 cup apricot nectar

1/4 cup chutney, chop large
  pieces

3 tablespoons dry sherry <u>or</u>
  water

2 tablespoons cornstarch

1/4 teaspoon salt

Chicken
2 tablespoons vegetable oil

2 teaspoons finely chopped
  fresh gingerroot*

2 (12 ounces each) whole
  boneless chicken breasts,
  skinned, cut into 1-inch
  cubes

Fruit
2 medium (2 cups) tart
  apples, cored, cut into
  1/4-inch slices

1 medium (1 cup) orange,
  peeled, sectioned

1/2 cup toasted slivered
  almonds

In small bowl stir together all sauce ingredients; set aside. In wok or 10-inch skillet heat oil; add gingerroot. (Add more oil as needed during stir-frying.) Cook over medium high heat, stirring constantly, 15 seconds. Add chicken to hot wok; continue cooking, stirring constantly, until chicken is fork tender (3 to 5 minutes). Push chicken from center of wok. Stir sauce; add sauce and apples to center of wok. Cook, stirring constantly, until thickened and apples are crisply tender (1 to 2 minutes). Add orange and almonds; stir to coat with sauce. Continue cooking, stirring constantly, until heated through (1 minute). **YIELD:** 4 servings.

* $1/2$ teaspoon ground ginger can be substituted for 2 teaspoons finely chopped fresh gingerroot.

Nutrition Information (1 serving): Calories 500; Protein 40g; Carbohydrate 39g; Fat 19g; Cholesterol 100mg; Sodium 380mg

Oyster-Sauced Chicken Stir-Fry

*This delectable stir-fry gets its delicate flavor from bottled oyster sauce,
a thick brown sauce made from oysters cooked in soy sauce.*

Preparation time: 30 minutes • Cooking time: 13 minutes

Sauce

2/3	cup water
1/3	cup oyster sauce
2	tablespoons dry white wine or chicken broth
1	tablespoon cornstarch
1	teaspoon sugar

Vegetables

3 to 4	tablespoons vegetable oil
2	teaspoons finely chopped fresh garlic
2	teaspoons finely chopped fresh gingerroot*
4	cups broccoli flowerets
2	(8-ounce) packages (4 cups) fresh mushrooms, sliced
1	(8-ounce) can sliced bamboo shoots, drained

Chicken

2	(12 ounces each) whole boneless chicken breasts, skinned, cut into 1/2-inch strips
2	cups hot cooked rice

In small bowl stir together all sauce ingredients; set aside. In wok or Dutch oven heat oil; add garlic and gingerroot. (Add more oil as needed during stir-frying.) Cook over medium high heat, stirring constantly, 15 seconds. Add broccoli; continue cooking, stirring constantly, 3 minutes. Add mushrooms and bamboo shoots; continue cooking, stirring constantly, until vegetables are crisply tender (1 to 2 minutes). Remove vegetables from wok; set aside. Add chicken to hot wok; cook over medium high heat, stirring constantly, until chicken is fork tender (3 to 5 minutes). Push chicken from center of wok. Stir sauce; add sauce to center of wok. Cook, stirring constantly, until slightly thickened (1 to 2 minutes). Return cooked vegetables to wok; stir to coat with sauce. Cook, stirring constantly, until heated through (1 minute). Serve over rice. **YIELD:** 4 servings.

* 1/2 teaspoon ground ginger can be substituted for 2 teaspoons finely chopped fresh gingerroot.

Nutrition Information (1 serving): Calories 520; Protein 47g; Carbohydrate 48g; Fat 16g; Cholesterol 100mg; Sodium 2830mg

Asparagus-Chicken Stir-Fry

This aromatic, tangy stir-fry spotlights the best of springtime vegetables with tender green asparagus and fresh mushrooms in a delicate lemon and basil sauce.

Preparation time: 30 minutes • Cooking time: 14 minutes

Sauce

- ¹/₃ cup water
- 2 teaspoons cornstarch
- ¹/₄ teaspoon salt
- ¹/₄ teaspoon coarsely ground pepper
- 1 tablespoon chopped fresh basil leaves*
- ¹/₂ teaspoon grated lemon peel
- 2 tablespoons lemon juice

Vegetables

- 2 to 3 tablespoons olive <u>or</u> vegetable oil
- 1 pound (24) fresh asparagus spears, cut into 2-inch pieces
- 1 large onion, cut into thin wedges
- 3 cups sliced fresh mushrooms
- ¹/₂ cup sun-dried tomatoes in olive oil, cut into ¹/₄-inch strips

Chicken

- 2 (12 ounces each) whole boneless chicken breasts, skinned, cut into ¹/₂-inch strips
- 1 tablespoon toasted sesame seed

In small bowl stir together all sauce ingredients; set aside. In wok or 10-inch skillet heat oil; add asparagus and onion. (Add more oil as needed during stir-frying.) Cook over medium high heat, stirring constantly, 4 minutes. Add mushrooms and tomatoes; continue cooking, stirring constantly, until asparagus is crisply tender (1 to 2 minutes). Remove vegetables from wok; set aside. Place chicken in hot wok; cook over medium high heat, stirring constantly, until chicken is fork tender (3 to 5 minutes). Push chicken from center of wok. Stir sauce; add sauce to center of wok. Cook, stirring constantly, until thickened (1 to 2 minutes). Return cooked vegetables to wok; stir to coat with sauce. Cook, stirring constantly, until heated through (1 minute). Place on serving plate; sprinkle with sesame seed.
YIELD: 4 servings.

* 1 teaspoon dried basil leaves can be substituted for 1 tablespoon chopped fresh basil leaves.

Nutrition Information (1 serving): Calories 340; Protein 41g; Carbohydrate 18g; Fat 14g; Cholesterol 100mg; Sodium 240mg

Skillet Chicken & Potato Dinner

Tender chicken breasts prepared with hearty vegetables.

Preparation time: 15 minutes • Cooking time: 38 minutes

3 tablespoons
  LAND O LAKES® Butter

1 teaspoon finely chopped
  fresh garlic

6 new red potatoes, quartered

1 medium onion, cut into
  6 wedges

3 (12 ounces each) whole
  boneless chicken breasts,
  skinned, halved

1 (10-ounce) package frozen
  whole green beans*

1/2 teaspoon salt

1/4 teaspoon pepper

1/4 cup chopped fresh parsley

In 10-inch skillet melt butter until sizzling; stir in garlic. Add potatoes and onion; cook over medium high heat, stirring occasionally, until browned (12 to 14 minutes). Remove from skillet; keep warm. Place chicken in same skillet. Cook over medium high heat, turning once, until fork tender and browned (10 to 12 minutes). Remove chicken from skillet; keep warm. Place potato mixture, green beans, salt and pepper in same skillet. Cover; cook over medium high heat, stirring occasionally, until beans are crisply tender (6 to 9 minutes). Add chicken and parsley. Continue cooking, stirring occasionally, until heated through (1 to 3 minutes). **YIELD:** 6 servings.

* 1 (10-ounce) package frozen cut green beans can be substituted for 1 (10-ounce) package frozen whole green beans.

Nutrition Information (1 serving): Calories 260; Protein 29g; Carbohydrate 15g; Fat 9g; Cholesterol 90mg; Sodium 310mg

Cheesy Tomato Basil Chicken Breasts

*Fresh tomatoes, basil and Mozzarella cheese make
chicken extra special.*

Preparation time: 20 minutes • Baking time: 56 minutes

Sauce

3   tablespoons
    LAND O LAKES® Butter

1/3 cup chopped onion

2   medium (2 cups) ripe
    tomatoes, cubed 1-inch

1   (6-ounce) can tomato paste

1   tablespoon dried basil
    leaves

1/2 teaspoon salt

1/4 teaspoon pepper

2   teaspoons finely chopped
    fresh garlic

Chicken

3   (12 ounces each) whole
    boneless chicken breasts,
    skinned, cut in half

Topping

3/4 cup fresh bread crumbs

1/4 cup chopped fresh parsley

2   tablespoons
    LAND O LAKES® Butter,
    melted

6   ounces (1 1/2 cups)
    LAND O LAKES®
    Mozzarella cheese,
    shredded

Heat oven to 350°. In 13x9-inch baking pan melt 3 tablespoons butter in oven (4 to 6 minutes). Meanwhile, in medium bowl stir together all remaining sauce ingredients; set aside. Place chicken in baking pan, turning to coat with butter. Spoon sauce mixture over chicken. Bake for 30 to 40 minutes or until chicken is no longer pink. Meanwhile, in small bowl stir together all topping ingredients <u>except</u> cheese. Sprinkle chicken with cheese; sprinkle with topping mixture. Continue baking for 5 to 10 minutes or until chicken is fork tender and bread crumbs are browned. **YIELD:** 6 servings.

*Nutrition Information (1 serving): Calories 420; Protein 47g; Carbohydrate 15g; Fat 19g;
Cholesterol 140mg; Sodium 780mg*

Orange Oregano Chicken

*You'll find just the right touch of orange and oregano
in this easy and delicious marinade.*

Preparation time: 15 minutes • Marinating time: 4 hours • Broiling time: 14 minutes

Marinade

$1/3$ cup finely chopped onion

$1/2$ cup orange juice

$1/4$ cup dry sherry <u>or</u> orange
juice

$1/4$ cup vegetable oil

$1/4$ teaspoon coarsely ground
pepper

4 teaspoons chopped fresh
oregano leaves*

1 tablespoon grated orange
peel

Chicken

2 (12 ounces each) whole
boneless chicken breasts,
skinned, halved

In large plastic food bag combine all marinade ingredients; add chicken breasts. Tightly seal bag. Turn bag several times to coat chicken. Place in 13x9-inch pan. Refrigerate, turning occasionally, at least 4 hours or overnight. Remove chicken from marinade. In 1-quart saucepan bring marinade to a full boil. <u>Heat broiler</u>. Place chicken on greased broiler pan. Broil 6 to 8 inches from heat, turning occasionally and basting with marinade, until chicken is fork tender (12 to 14 minutes).
YIELD: 4 servings.

<u>Grilling Directions</u>: Prepare grill placing coals to one side; heat until coals are ash white. Make aluminum foil drip pan; place opposite coals. Place chicken on grill over drip pan. Grill, turning and basting occasionally with marinade, until chicken is fork tender (40 to 50 minutes).

* $1^1/2$ teaspoons dried oregano leaves can be substituted for 4 teaspoons chopped fresh oregano leaves.

*Nutrition Information (1 serving): Calories 270; Protein 37g; Carbohydrate 3g; Fat 11g;
Cholesterol 100mg; Sodium 90mg*

Chicken *with* Mushroom Cilantro Sauce

*Chicken fans will applaud this rich and creamy mushroom-leek sauce
served over buttered noodles.*

Preparation time: 20 minutes • Broiling time: 35 minutes • Cooking time: 8 minutes

Chicken

2 tablespoons
   LAND O LAKES® Butter,
   melted
1 tablespoon lemon juice
2 (16 ounces each) whole
   chicken breasts, halved

Sauce

2 tablespoons
   LAND O LAKES® Butter
1/2 cup thinly sliced leeks <u>or</u>
   green onions
1 (8-ounce) package (2 cups)
   fresh mushrooms
2 tablespoons all-purpose
   flour
1 cup chicken broth
1/4 cup chopped fresh cilantro
   <u>or</u> parsley
1/4 cup half-and-half <u>or</u> milk
1/4 teaspoon pepper

3 cups buttered hot cooked
   noodles

In small bowl combine 2 tablespoons butter and lemon juice. <u>Heat broiler</u>. Place chicken on greased broiler pan. Broil 6 to 8 inches from heat, turning every 10 minutes and basting with lemon butter mixture, until chicken is fork tender (30 to 35 minutes). Meanwhile, in 2-quart saucepan melt 2 tablespoons butter until sizzling; stir in leeks and mushrooms. Cook over medium heat, stirring occasionally, until vegetables are crisply tender (2 to 3 minutes). Stir in flour. Add chicken broth. Continue cooking, stirring constantly, until thickened (2 to 3 minutes). Reduce heat to low. In small bowl combine cilantro, half-and-half and pepper; stir into mushroom mixture. Continue cooking, stirring constantly, until thickened (1 to 2 minutes). Serve sauce over chicken and noodles. **YIELD:** 4 servings.

<u>Grilling Directions</u>: Prepare grill placing coals to one side; heat until coals are ash white. Make aluminum foil drip pan; place opposite coals. Place chicken on grill over drip pan. Grill, turning and basting occasionally with lemon butter mixture, until chicken is fork tender (40 to 50 minutes).

*Nutrition Information (1 serving): Calories 520; Protein 41g; Carbohydrate 39g; Fat 22g;
Cholesterol 170mg; Sodium 440mg*

Crab & Mushroom Chicken Breasts

A hint of tarragon adds the ultimate in flavor to tender chicken breasts cooked with carrot strips, mushrooms and crab in a subtle wine sauce.

Preparation time: 20 minutes • Cooking time: 19 minutes

^{2}/$_3$ cup LAND O LAKES® Butter

4 (12 ounces each) whole boneless chicken breasts, skinned, halved

2 medium (1 cup) carrots, cut into 2x^1/$_4$-inch strips

1 cup sliced ^{1}/$_4$-inch fresh mushrooms

1 (6-ounce) package frozen crab, thawed, drained

^{1}/$_4$ cup chopped fresh parsley

^{1}/$_4$ cup white wine <u>or</u> apple juice

^{1}/$_2$ teaspoon salt

^{1}/$_2$ teaspoon dried tarragon leaves

Paprika

In 10-inch skillet melt butter until sizzling; add chicken breasts and carrots. Cook over medium heat until chicken is lightly browned (5 to 7 minutes). Turn chicken breasts over. Stir in all remaining ingredients <u>except</u> paprika. Continue cooking, stirring occasionally, until chicken is fork tender (9 to 12 minutes). To serve, sprinkle with paprika. **YIELD:** 8 servings.

Nutrition Information (1 serving): Calories 360; Protein 41g; Carbohydrate 2g; Fat 20g; Cholesterol 150mg; Sodium 560mg

Braised Tarragon Chicken

Tarragon's flavor blends well with chicken to create a light, fresh taste.

Preparation time: 15 minutes • Cooking time: 37 minutes

3   tablespoons
    LAND O LAKES® Butter

2   teaspoons finely chopped
    fresh garlic

1   teaspoon dried tarragon
    leaves

4   (12 ounces each) whole
    boneless chicken breasts,
    skinned, halved

1/2 cup white wine <u>or</u> chicken
    broth

4   medium carrots, sliced
    1/4-inch

1/2 teaspoon salt

1/4 teaspoon pepper

1   medium red onion, cut into
    eighths

1   teaspoon cornstarch

1   teaspoon cold water

1/4 cup chopped fresh parsley

In 10-inch skillet melt butter until sizzling; stir in garlic and tarragon. Add chicken breasts. Cook over medium high heat, stirring occasionally, until chicken is lightly browned (3 to 5 minutes). Reduce heat to medium. Stir in all remaining ingredients <u>except</u> onion, cornstarch, water and parsley. Cover; cook, stirring occasionally, until chicken is fork tender (15 to 20 minutes). Add onion; continue cooking until onion is tender (5 to 7 minutes). In small bowl stir together cornstarch and cold water; stir into hot chicken mixture. Continue cooking, stirring occasionally, until mixture thickens (3 to 5 minutes). Sprinkle with parsley. **YIELD:** 8 servings.

Nutrition Information (1 serving): Calories 270; Protein 37g; Carbohydrate 6g; Fat 9g; Cholesterol 110mg; Sodium 280mg

Pico de Gallo Chicken Breast Sandwiches

Mexican flavors are highlighted in this marinated chicken sandwich.

Preparation time: 30 minutes • Marinating time: 1 hour • Grilling time: 12 minutes

Pico de Gallo Sauce

1/2 cup chopped fresh
 cilantro

1/2 cup finely chopped red
 onion

1/4 teaspoon sugar

2 medium (2 cups) ripe
 tomatoes, chopped

2 tablespoons finely chopped
 fresh garlic

4 teaspoons finely chopped
 seeded jalapeño peppers

1 teaspoon grated lime peel

1 tablespoon lime juice

1 tablespoon vegetable oil

Sandwiches

1 cup pico de gallo sauce

1/3 cup lime juice

1/4 cup vegetable oil

3 (12 ounces each) whole
 boneless chicken breasts,
 skinned, halved

6 hoagie buns

LAND O LAKES® Light Sour
 Cream, if desired

In medium bowl stir together all pico de gallo sauce ingredients; reserve 1 cup. Cover; refrigerate remaining sauce. In large plastic food bag combine reserved 1 cup pico de gallo sauce, 1/3 cup lime juice, 1/4 cup oil and chicken breasts; tightly seal bag. Turn bag several times to coat chicken well. Place in 13x9-inch pan. Refrigerate 1 hour. Meanwhile, prepare grill; heat until coals are ash white. Remove chicken from marinade; discard marinade. Place chicken on grill. Grill, turning once, until chicken is fork tender (8 to 12 minutes). Serve chicken in hoagie buns with about 1/4 cup pico de gallo sauce and dollop of sour cream. **YIELD:** 6 sandwiches (1 1/2 cups sauce).

Broiling Directions: Heat broiler. Place chicken on broiler pan. Broil 6 to 8 inches from heat, turning occasionally and basting with marinade, until chicken is fork tender (12 to 14 minutes).

Nutrition Information (1 sandwich): Calories 300; Protein 28g; Carbohydrate 26g; Fat 9g; Cholesterol 70mg; Sodium 270mg

Picnic Drumsticks

*Onion crispy drumsticks are served hot or cold with
a fresh sour cream-cucumber dip.*

Preparation time: 20 minutes • Baking time: 55 minutes

Chicken

1/3 cup LAND O LAKES®
   Butter
1/3 cup crushed saltine
   crackers
2 tablespoons onion soup mix
8 chicken legs

Dip

1 cup LAND O LAKES®
   Light Sour Cream
1 medium (1 cup) cucumber,
   peeled, chopped
1 1/2 teaspoons chopped
   fresh chives
1/2 teaspoon salt
1/2 teaspoon dried dill weed

Heat oven to 350°. In 13x9-inch baking pan melt butter in oven (5 to 7 minutes). Stir together crushed crackers and onion soup mix. Dip chicken legs into melted butter, then coat with crumb mixture. In same pan place chicken legs; sprinkle with remaining crumb mixture. Bake for 45 to 55 minutes or until fork tender. Meanwhile, in medium bowl stir together all dip ingredients. Cover; refrigerate at least 1 hour. Serve chicken hot or cold with dip. **YIELD:** 4 servings (1^1/3 cups dip).

Nutrition Information (1 serving): Calories 410; Protein 30g; Carbohydrate 15g; Fat 25g; Cholesterol 130mg; Sodium 1110mg

One-Pan Chicken Dinner

Noodles and frozen green beans are cooked in the same skillet with chicken; a true meal-in-a-pan.

Preparation time: 10 minutes • Cooking time: 50 minutes

3 tablespoons
  LAND O LAKES® Butter

1 teaspoon finely chopped
  fresh garlic

3 pounds chicken legs

2 cups chicken broth

1/2 cup water

3 cups uncooked dried egg
  noodles

1 (16-ounce) package frozen
  cut green beans

1/2 teaspoon salt

1/4 teaspoon pepper

1/4 teaspoon dried thyme leaves

1 medium red onion, cut into
  8 wedges

In Dutch oven melt butter until sizzling; stir in garlic. Add chicken. Cook over medium high heat, stirring occasionally, until chicken is light golden brown (10 to 15 minutes). Stir in chicken broth and water. Continue cooking, stirring occasionally, until chicken is no longer pink (10 to 15 minutes). Reduce heat to medium; stir in all remaining ingredients <u>except</u> onion. Cover; cook, stirring occasionally, until chicken and noodles are fork tender (10 to 15 minutes). Stir in onion. Cover; continue cooking until onion is tender (5 minutes). Let stand 5 minutes. **YIELD:** 6 servings.

Nutrition Information (1 serving): Calories 320; Protein 28g; Carbohydrate 21g; Fat 14g; Cholesterol 110mg; Sodium 580mg

Garlic Chicken *with* Roasted Peppers

Crisp salad greens and Italian bread make great accompaniments for broiled garlic chicken.

Preparation time: 15 minutes • Broiling time: 40 minutes

1   teaspoon chopped fresh
     thyme leaves*

$^1/_2$ teaspoon salt

$^1/_2$ teaspoon coarsely ground
     pepper

2   teaspoons finely chopped
     fresh garlic

3   tablespoons olive <u>or</u>
     vegetable oil

1   (3 to 4-pound) frying
     chicken, cut into 8 pieces

1   medium onion, cut into
     wedges

1   medium red pepper, cut into
     2-inch pieces

1   medium yellow pepper, cut
     into 2-inch pieces

Heat broiler. In small bowl stir together thyme, salt, pepper, garlic and oil. Spray broiler pan with no stick cooking spray. On broiler pan place chicken and vegetables; brush with oil mixture. Broil 4 to 6 inches from heat, turning once, until chicken is fork tender (35 to 40 minutes). (Parts of peppers and onion will blacken.) **YIELD:** 6 servings.

* $^1/_4$ teaspoon dried thyme leaves can be substituted for 1 teaspoon chopped fresh thyme leaves.

Nutrition Information (1 serving): Calories 210; Protein 22g; Carbohydrate 4g; Fat 12g; Cholesterol 65mg; Sodium 240mg

Southern Fried Peanut Chicken

*The family is sure to gather at the table for this fried chicken
with a crunchy peanut gravy.*

Preparation time: 45 minutes • Cooking time: 30 minutes

Chicken

- ¹/₂ cup all-purpose flour
- ¹/₂ teaspoon salt
- ¹/₄ teaspoon pepper
- ¹/₂ cup shortening
- 1 (3 to 4-pound) frying
    chicken, cut into 8 pieces

Gravy

- ¹/₂ cup sliced ¹/₄-inch green
    onions
- ¹/₂ cup crunchy-style peanut
    butter
- 1¹/₄ cups milk
- ¹/₄ teaspoon pepper
- ¹/₄ cup salted peanuts

In 9-inch pie pan stir together flour, salt and ¹/₄ teaspoon pepper. Coat chicken pieces with flour mixture. In 10-inch skillet melt shortening. Place <u>4</u> chicken pieces in hot shortening. Cover; cook over medium high heat, turning occasionally, until chicken is golden brown and fork tender (20 to 25 minutes). Place fried chicken on platter; keep warm while frying remaining chicken. Pour off fat from skillet; <u>reserve brown particles</u>. Add all gravy ingredients <u>except</u> peanuts. Cook over medium heat, stirring occasionally, until gravy is thickened (4 to 5 minutes). Serve gravy over fried chicken; sprinkle with peanuts.
YIELD: 6 servings.

*Nutrition Information (1 serving): Calories 490; Protein 27g; Carbohydrate 17g; Fat 36g;
Cholesterol 60mg; Sodium 390mg*

Garden Vegetable Skillet Dinner

Thyme's aromatic flavor blends well with garden-fresh vegetables in this skillet dinner.

Preparation time: 20 minutes • Cooking time: 48 minutes

1 (3 to 4-pound) frying chicken, cut into 8 pieces

$^1/_3$ cup all-purpose flour

3 tablespoons LAND O LAKES® Butter

$^1/_4$ cup water

4 medium carrots, cut into 1-inch pieces

1 medium onion, cut into eighths

1 teaspoon salt

1 teaspoon dried thyme leaves

$^1/_4$ teaspoon pepper

2 cups broccoli flowerets

Coat chicken with flour. In 10-inch skillet melt butter until sizzling; add chicken. Cook over high heat, turning once, until golden brown (8 to 10 minutes). Reduce heat to medium. Add all remaining ingredients <u>except</u> broccoli. Cover; continue cooking until chicken is fork tender (20 to 30 minutes). Add broccoli. Cover; continue cooking until broccoli is crisply tender (5 to 8 minutes). **YIELD:** 6 servings.

Nutrition Information (1 serving): Calories 230; Protein 20g; Carbohydrate 13g; Fat 11g; Cholesterol 70mg; Sodium 490mg

Herb Butter Roasted Chicken

Rosemary, fresh parsley and garlic create a savory roasted chicken.

Preparation time: 10 minutes • Baking time: 2 hours 30 minutes

Chicken

1 (4 to 5-pound) whole
   roasting chicken

Herb Rub

$^1/_4$ cup LAND O LAKES®
   Butter, softened

1 teaspoon dried rosemary,
   crushed

1 teaspoon salt

$^1/_4$ teaspoon pepper

2 tablespoons chopped fresh
   parsley

1 teaspoon finely chopped
   fresh garlic

Heat oven to 350°. Secure wings and legs to body of chicken. In small bowl stir together all herb rub ingredients; rub onto chicken. Place chicken, breast side up, on rack in roasting pan. Bake for 2 to $2^1/_2$ hours or until fork tender. **YIELD:** 6 servings.

VARIATION

Herb Butter Roasted Chicken with Vegetables: Double ingredients for Herb Rub. Rub half onto chicken; <u>reserve remaining half</u>. Place 6 new red potatoes, cut in half; 6 carrots, cut in half crosswise and 2 medium onions, cut into quarters, on bottom of pan around chicken. Dollop reserved herb rub evenly over vegetables. Baste chicken and vegetables occasionally during baking time.

Nutrition Information (1 serving): Calories 290; Protein 38g; Carbohydrate <1g; Fat 14g; Cholesterol 120mg; Sodium 330mg

Orange Roasted Chicken

This moist, light orange stuffing flavors the whole chicken.
Serve with fresh asparagus and whole wheat rolls.

Preparation time: 30 minutes • Cooking time: 4 minutes • Baking time: 2 hours 30 minutes

Stuffing

1½	cups dried bread cubes
¼	cup chopped onion
¼	cup LAND O LAKES® Butter, melted
2	stalks (1 cup) celery, sliced ½-inch
1	(11-ounce) can mandarin oranges, drained
½	teaspoon salt
¼	teaspoon pepper
⅛	teaspoon ginger
2	tablespoons orange juice

Chicken

1	(4 to 5-pound) whole roasting chicken

Glaze

⅓	cup orange marmalade
⅛	teaspoon ginger
2	tablespoons white wine <u>or</u> orange juice

Heat oven to 350°. In medium bowl stir together all stuffing ingredients. Stuff chicken. Secure wings and legs to body of chicken. Place chicken, breast side up, on rack in roasting pan. In 1-quart saucepan combine all glaze ingredients. Cook over medium high heat, stirring constantly, until heated through (3 to 4 minutes). Spoon glaze over chicken. Bake, basting occasionally, for 1 hour. If needed, add water to basting juices. Loosely cover chicken with aluminum foil. Continue baking, basting occasionally, for 1½ hours or until chicken is fork tender. **YIELD:** 6 servings.

Nutrition Information (1 serving): Calories 430; Protein 40g; Carbohydrate 26g; Fat 18g; Cholesterol 140mg; Sodium 460mg

Layered Chicken Casserole

Prepare this casserole the night before your next brunch. Serve with fresh berries and bran muffins for a feast that is easy on the cook.

Preparation time: 20 minutes • Chilling time: 8 hours • Baking time: 1 hour 30 minutes

1 (12 to 14-ounce package) (6 cups) dried cubed herb seasoned stuffing

2 cups cubed 1-inch cooked chicken

2 cups frozen broccoli flowerets

1 (10 3/4-ounce) can condensed cream of chicken soup

1 (10 3/4-ounce) can condensed cream of mushroom soup

2 (2-ounce) jars chopped pimiento

1 cup (4 ounces) LAND O LAKES® Cheddar Cheese, shredded

2 cups milk

4 eggs, slightly beaten

1/4 teaspoon pepper

2 tablespoons LAND O LAKES® Butter, melted

Spread <u>3 cups</u> dried stuffing on bottom of greased 13x9-inch baking pan; set aside. In large bowl stir together chicken, broccoli, mushroom soup, chicken soup and pimiento. Spoon over stuffing; sprinkle with cheese. In medium bowl combine all remaining ingredients <u>except</u> 3 cups dried stuffing and butter. Pour over chicken mixture. Cover; refrigerate 8 hours or overnight. <u>Heat oven to 350°</u>. Sprinkle with 3 cups remaining dried stuffing; drizzle with butter. Bake for 1 to 1½ hours or until set and heated through. **YIELD:** 6 servings.

Nutrition Information (1 serving): Calories 610; Protein 36g; Carbohydrate 56g; Fat 28g; Cholesterol 230mg; Sodium 1860mg

Starburst Casserole

*Slices of bread cut into stars top this
kid-pleasing chicken casserole.*

Preparation time: 30 minutes • Baking time: 1 hour

6 slices white bread
1/2 cup LAND O LAKES®
   Butter
2 cups cubed cooked chicken
   or turkey
8 ounces (2 cups)
   LAND O LAKES®
   American Cheese, shredded
1 (10-ounce) package frozen
   mixed vegetables, thawed,
   drained
2 (10-3/4 ounce) cans
   condensed cream of
   mushroom soup
1/2 teaspoon dried dill weed

Heat oven to 350°. In 13x9-inch baking dish melt butter in oven (4 to 5 minutes). Meanwhile, with $2^1/2$-inch star shaped cookie cutter cut 2 stars from each slice of bread. Dip 1 side of each star into melted butter; set stars aside. Crumble remaining bread from slices (a blender or food processor works well). Stir crumbs into remaining butter in dish. Press lightly on bottom of baking dish to form crust. In large bowl stir together all remaining ingredients. Spread over crust. Top with stars, butter-side up. Bake for 50 to 60 minutes or until bubbly around edges and stars are toasted. **YIELD:** 10 servings.

Nutrition Information (1 serving): Calories 340; Protein 17g; Carbohydrate 17g; Fat 24g; Cholesterol 70mg; Sodium 1040mg

Mediterranean Chicken Soup

*This hearty, warming soup features fresh
fennel and black olives.*

Preparation time: 30 minutes • Cooking time: 28 minutes

Stock

- $1/2$ cup orange juice
- 3 ($10^1/2$-ounce) cans chicken broth
- 1 (8-ounce) can stewed tomatoes
- 4 medium (2 cups) carrots, sliced
- 2 medium (1 cup) onions, chopped
- 1 bulb (1 cup) fresh fennel, trimmed, thinly sliced
- $1/4$ teaspoon salt
- $1/8$ to $1/4$ teaspoon dried red pepper flakes
- 1 tablespoon chopped fresh basil leaves*
- 1 tablespoon chopped fresh thyme leaves**
- 1 teaspoon finely chopped fresh garlic

Chicken

- 2 cups cubed 1-inch cooked chicken
- 1 ($2^1/4$-ounce) can ($1/2$ cup) sliced ripe olives, drained
- $1/4$ cup chopped fresh parsley

In Dutch oven combine all stock ingredients. Cook over high heat until mixture comes to a full boil (8 to 10 minutes). Cook over medium high heat, stirring occasionally, 15 minutes. Stir in chicken and olives; continue cooking until heated through (2 to 3 minutes). Ladle into individual serving bowls. Sprinkle each serving with parsley.

YIELD: 4 servings.

* 1 teaspoon dried basil leaves can be substituted for 1 tablespoon chopped fresh basil leaves.

** 1 teaspoon dried thyme leaves can be substituted for 1 tablespoon chopped fresh thyme leaves.

Nutrition Information (1 serving): Calories 270; Protein 27g; Carbohydrate 21g; Fat 9g; Cholesterol 60mg; Sodium 1230mg

Chicken & Shrimp Pasta Soup

Enjoy this simply elegant way of serving chicken. It's based on a light consommé seasoned with a bit of lemon grass and gingerroot.

Preparation time: 20 minutes • Cooking time: 23 minutes

Stock

1/2 cup green onion slivers <u>or</u> chopped green onions

3 (14½-ounce) cans chicken broth

2 ounces uncooked dried vermicelli <u>or</u> thin spaghetti, broken in half

2 medium (1 cup) carrots, diagonally sliced ¼-inch

2 stalks (1 tablespoon) fresh lemon grass, finely chopped*

1 teaspoon finely chopped fresh gingerroot**

Chicken

1½ cups cubed 1-inch cooked chicken

4 ounces fresh <u>or</u> frozen medium shrimp, peeled, deveined

1 medium avocado, pitted, peeled, cut into ½-inch slices

In Dutch oven combine all stock ingredients. Cook over high heat until mixture comes to a full boil (8 to 10 minutes). Reduce heat to medium high. Continue cooking, stirring occasionally, 10 minutes. Stir in chicken and shrimp. Continue cooking until heated through (2 to 3 minutes). Ladle into individual serving bowls. Top each serving with avocado slices. **YIELD:** 4 servings.

* ½ teaspoon grated lemon peel can be substituted for 2 stalks (1 tablespoon) fresh lemon grass, finely chopped.

**⅛ teaspoon ground ginger can be substituted for 1 teaspoon finely chopped fresh gingerroot.

TIP: To make green onion slivers, trim to 3-inch lengths. Lay on cutting board; using a sharp paring knife, cut lengthwise into thin slices.

Nutrition Information (1 serving): Calories 320; Protein 29g; Carbohydrate 19g; Fat 14g; Cholesterol 80mg; Sodium 1070mg

Chicken & Greens
Topped *with* Blue Cheese

Serve this beautiful, yet hearty, salad all year 'round.

Preparation time: 45 minutes • Chilling time: 1 hour

Dressing

$^1/_4$ cup finely chopped onion

$^1/_4$ cup chopped sun-dried
   tomatoes in olive oil

$^1/_4$ cup olive <u>or</u> vegetable oil

$^1/_4$ cup balsamic vinegar

1 tablespoon chopped fresh
   marjoram leaves*

1 teaspoon sugar

$^1/_2$ teaspoon crushed
   red pepper

Salad

1 head (7 cups) red-tip leaf
   lettuce, torn

1 cup torn radicchio**

1$^1/_2$ cups cubed 1-inch cooked
   chicken

2 medium carrots, thinly
   sliced

1 (8-ounce) package (2 cups)
   fresh mushrooms, sliced

$^1/_2$ cup (2 ounces) crumbled
   blue cheese

In jar with tight-fitting lid combine all dressing ingredients; shake well. Refrigerate 1 hour. In large serving bowl combine all salad ingredients <u>except</u> blue cheese. Shake dressing well; pour over salad mixture. Toss lightly to coat. Place salad on 4 plates; sprinkle with blue cheese.
YIELD: 4 servings.

* 1 teaspoon dried marjoram leaves can be substituted for 1 tablespoon chopped fresh marjoram leaves.

** 1 cup shredded red cabbage can be substituted for 1 cup torn radicchio.

Nutrition Information (1 serving): Calories 350; Protein 22g; Carbohydrate 16g; Fat 23g; Cholesterol 60mg; Sodium 270mg

Fruited Chicken & Greens Salad
with Blueberry Dressing

*Puréed blueberries are the base of a unique citrus dressing
served over greens, chicken, and fruit.*

Preparation time: 45 minutes • Chilling time: 2 hours

Dressing

  1 pint (2 cups) fresh <u>or</u> frozen
      blueberries

 ¼ cup orange-flavored liqueur
      <u>or</u> orange juice

 ¼ cup lemon <u>or</u> lime juice

  1 tablespoon honey

 ⅓ cup vegetable oil

  1 tablespoon chopped fresh
      basil leaves*

Salad

  8 cups torn romaine lettuce <u>or</u>
      mixed salad greens

1½ cups cubed 1-inch cooked
      chicken

1½ cups seedless grapes, halved

 ½ small (2 cups) pineapple,
      peeled, cored, cut into
      1-inch cubes**

  2 kiwi fruit, peeled, sliced,
      halved

In 5-cup blender container or food processor bowl combine <u>1 cup</u> blueberries and all remaining dressing ingredients <u>except</u> basil. Cover; blend at High speed until blueberries are pureed. Strain mixture to remove blueberry skins; discard skins. In container with tight-fitting lid combine blueberry mixture and basil; shake well. Refrigerate 2 hours. In large bowl combine remaining 1 cup blueberries and all salad ingredients. Shake dressing well. Serve dressing with salad.
YIELD: 4 servings.

*1 teaspoon dried basil leaves can be substituted for 1 tablespoon chopped fresh basil leaves.

** 1 (15½-ounce) can pineapple chunks, drained, can be substituted for ½ small (2 cups) pineapple, peeled, cored, cut into 1-inch cubes.

Nutrition Information (1 serving): Calories 520; Protein 19g; Carbohydrate 55g; Fat 24g; Cholesterol 45mg; Sodium 70mg

great *Grilling!*

Spicy Cajun Shrimp and
Grilled Ham with Apple Chutney

Spicy Cajun Shrimp

A spicy Cajun sauce complements fresh shrimp.

Preparation time: 20 minutes • Grilling time: 6 minutes (pictured on page 134)

Sauce

- 1/4 cup LAND O LAKES® Butter
- 1 teaspoon chopped fresh thyme leaves*
- 1/2 teaspoon pepper
- 1/8 to 1/4 teaspoon ground red pepper
- 2 tablespoons ketchup
- 1 teaspoon Worcestershire sauce
- 1/2 teaspoon finely chopped fresh garlic

Kabobs

- 1 pound (20 to 25) fresh raw shrimp, cleaned, shelled, deveined
- 8 green onions, each cut into 3 (2-inch) pieces
- 2 lemons, each cut into 6 slices, then cut in half

- 12 (6-inch) wooden skewers, soaked in water

Prepare grill; heat until coals are ash white.

Meanwhile, in 1-quart saucepan combine all sauce ingredients. Cook over medium heat, stirring occasionally, until butter is melted (4 to 5 minutes).

To assemble kabobs on each wooden skewer place 1 shrimp, 1 green onion piece, 1 lemon slice, 1 shrimp and 1 green onion piece; brush with sauce. Place kabobs on grill. Grill, brushing with sauce and turning frequently, until shrimp turn pink (6 to 10 minutes). **YIELD:** 4 servings.

* 1/4 teaspoon dried thyme leaves can be substituted for 1 teaspoon chopped fresh thyme leaves.

Nutrition Facts (1 serving): Calories 240; Protein 20g; Carbohydrate 12g; Fat 14g; Cholesterol 160mg; Sodium 340mg

Grilled Ham *with* Apple Chutney

Apple and raisin chutney served over ham steak.

Preparation time: 30 minutes • Cooking time: 1 hour 30 minutes • Grilling time: 6 minutes (pictured on page 135)

Chutney

$^1/_2$ lemon, pared, chopped

$^1/_2$ teaspoon finely chopped
    fresh garlic

2 medium ($2^1/_2$ cups) tart
    apples, cored, chopped

1 cup firmly packed brown
    sugar

1 cup raisins

1 teaspoon grated fresh
    gingerroot*

$^1/_2$ teaspoon salt

$^1/_8$ teaspoon ground red pepper

$^3/_4$ cup cider vinegar

Ham

$1^1/_2$ pound ($^1/_2$-inch thick) ham
    steak

In 2-quart saucepan combine all chutney ingredients. Cook over low heat, stirring occasionally, until chutney thickens (1 1/2 to 2 hours).

Prepare grill; heat coals until ash white. Place ham steak on grill. Grill until edges are lightly browned (3 to 4 minutes). Turn ham steak over; spread with 1/4 cup chutney. Continue grilling until heated through (3 to 4 minutes). Serve with additional warm chutney.

YIELD: 6 servings (2 cups chutney).

* 1/4 teaspoon ground ginger can be substituted for 1 teaspoon grated fresh gingerroot.

Nutrition Facts (1 serving): Calories 410; Protein 25g; Carbohydrate 66g; Fat 6g; Cholesterol 60mg; Sodium 1560mg

Grilled Steaks *with* Garden Tomato Basil Sauce

A wonderfully flavored fresh tomato sauce tastes good on steaks or other grilled meats.

Preparation time: 30 minutes • Marinating time: 20 minutes • Grilling time: 10 minutes

Marinade

- 1/4 cup vegetable oil
- 2 teaspoons dried oregano leaves
- 1/2 teaspoon coarsely ground pepper
- 1/8 teaspoon salt
- 2 tablespoons lemon juice

4 to 6 rib-eye *or* porterhouse beef steaks

Sauce

- 1/4 cup chopped red onion
- 2 medium (2 cups) ripe tomatoes, cubed 1/2-inch*
- 1 (6-ounce) can tomato paste
- 1 tablespoon chopped fresh basil leaves
- 1/8 teaspoon salt
- 1/8 teaspoon ground red pepper
- 2 tablespoons red wine vinegar
- 1 tablespoon lemon juice
- 1/2 teaspoon finely chopped fresh garlic

Prepare grill; heat until coals are ash white.

Meanwhile, in large plastic food bag place all marinade ingredients except rib-eye steaks; add steaks. Tightly seal bag. Turn bag several times to coat steaks well. Place in 13x9-inch pan; let stand 20 minutes.

Meanwhile, in medium bowl stir together all sauce ingredients. In 5-cup blender container place about 1 cup sauce mixture. Cover; blend on high speed until saucy (30 to 45 seconds). Stir back into sauce mixture. Set aside.

Remove steaks from marinade; reserve marinade. Place steaks on grill. Grill, basting with marinade and turning once, until desired doneness (10 to 15 minutes for medium). Serve sauce over steaks.
YIELD: 6 servings.

* 1 (16-ounce) can plum tomatoes can be substituted for 2 medium (2 cups) ripe tomatoes, cubed 1/2-inch.

Nutrition Facts (1 serving): Calories 330; Protein 33g; Carbohydrate 9g; Fat 18g; Cholesterol 90mg; Sodium 370mg

Sweet & Tangy Family Steak

The marinade enhances both the subtle flavor and the tenderness of this popular cut of meat.

Preparation time: 30 minutes • Marinating time: 6 hours • Grilling time: 13 minutes

Marinade

1/2 cup ketchup

1/4 cup country-style Dijon mustard

2 tablespoons firmly packed brown sugar

1/2 teaspoon coarsely ground pepper

1/4 teaspoon salt

1 teaspoon finely chopped fresh garlic

1 tablespoon cider vinegar

Steak

1 1/2 pound (1-inch thick) beef top round steak

In large plastic food bag place all marinade ingredients. Pierce round steak all over with fork; place steak in plastic food bag. Tightly seal bag. Turn bag several times to coat steak well. Place in 13x9-inch pan. Refrigerate at least 6 hours or overnight.

<u>Prepare grill</u> placing coals to one side; heat until coals are ash white. Make aluminum foil drip pan; place opposite coals. Place steak on grill over drip pan. Grill 8 minutes; turn. Brush with marinade; continue grilling until desired doneness (5 to 8 minutes).

Meanwhile, in 1-quart saucepan cook remaining marinade over medium heat until heated through (2 to 4 minutes). To serve, cut steak, on the diagonal, into thin slices. Serve with hot marinade. **YIELD:** 6 servings.

Nutrition Facts (1 serving): Calories 190; Protein 26g; Carbohydrate 12g; Fat 4g; Cholesterol 65mg; Sodium 530mg

Flank Steak *in* Fajita Marinade

A spicy marinade makes these beef fajitas especially tasty.

Preparation time: 30 minutes • Marinating time: 4 hours • Grilling time: 10 minutes

Marinade

1/2 cup lime juice

1/2 cup vegetable oil

1/3 cup chopped onion

1/4 cup chopped fresh
  cilantro

1 teaspoon ground cumin

1 teaspoon grated lime peel

1 teaspoon finely chopped
  seeded jalapeño pepper

1/4 teaspoon coarsely ground
  pepper

Fajita

1 1/2 pounds beef flank steak
  <u>or</u> skirt steak

1 tablespoon vegetable oil

1 green pepper, cut into
  2x1/4-inch strips

1 medium onion, cut into
  1/4-inch slices

12 (8-inch) flour tortillas,
  warmed

LAND O LAKES® Sour Cream

Guacamole

In large plastic food bag place all marinade ingredients; add flank steak. Tightly seal bag. Turn bag several times to coat steak well. Place in 13x9-inch pan. Refrigerate at least 4 hours or overnight.

<u>Prepare grill</u>; heat until coals are ash white. Remove steak from marinade. Place on grill. Grill, turning once, until steak is cooked to desired doneness (10 to 12 minutes). Slice across grain into 1/4-inch slices.

Meanwhile, in 8-inch skillet place 1 tablespoon oil, green pepper and onion slices. Cook over medium high heat, stirring occasionally, until vegetables are crisply tender (6 to 8 minutes). To serve, place steak slices and vegetables in center of each tortilla; top with sour cream and guacamole. **YIELD:** 6 servings.

Nutrition Facts (1 serving): Calories 560; Protein 31g; Carbohydrate 54g; Fat 25g; Cholesterol 60mg; Sodium 460mg

Cheddar Cheese–Pecan Rolled Flank Steak

Slice into this tender, marinated flank steak and discover a moist, flavorful stuffing.

Preparation time: 30 minutes • Marinating time: 6 hours • Grilling time: 40 minutes

Marinade

- 2 medium (1 cup) onions, chopped
- 2 cups pineapple juice
- 1 teaspoon salt
- 1 teaspoon dried thyme leaves
- 1/2 teaspoon pepper
- 1/2 teaspoon dried rosemary, crushed
- 2 tablespoons Worcestershire sauce

1 1/2 to 2 pounds beef flank steak

Stuffing

- 1 1/2 cups fresh bread crumbs
- 6 ounces (1 1/2 cups) LAND O LAKES® Cheddar Cheese, shredded
- 1/2 cup chopped pecans
- 1/4 cup chopped onion
- 1/4 cup chopped fresh parsley
- 1/2 teaspoon finely chopped fresh garlic

In large plastic food bag place all marinade ingredients <u>except</u> flank steak. With mallet, pound steak to 1/4-inch thickness. Place steak in large plastic food bag; tightly seal bag. Turn bag several times to coat steak well. Place in 13x9-inch baking pan. Refrigerate, turning twice, at least 6 hours or overnight.

<u>Prepare grill</u> placing coals to one side; heat until coals are ash white. Make aluminum foil drip pan; place opposite coals. Remove steak from marinade; <u>reserve marinade</u>.

In medium bowl combine all stuffing ingredients. Place stuffing mixture over entire surface of steak, pressing slightly. Tightly roll up steak, jelly roll fashion. Tie with string to secure filling inside roll. Place steak on grill directly over coals. Grill, turning to brown all sides, 10 minutes. Move steak and place over drip pan. Baste with reserved marinade. Cover; grill until desired doneness (30 to 40 minutes). **YIELD:** 8 servings.

Nutrition Facts (1 serving): Calories 330; Protein 25g; Carbohydrate 12g; Fat 20g; Cholesterol 70mg; Sodium 380mg

Beef Kabobs *with* Horseradish Sauce

Horseradish has a pungent, spicy flavor that tastes especially delicious with beef.

Preparation time: 30 minutes • Marinating time: 30 minutes • Grilling time: 10 minutes

Kabobs

1 pound beef sirloin, cut into
    about 32 (1-inch) pieces
1/4 cup Italian dressing
8 small fresh mushrooms
8 cherry tomatoes
1 small green pepper, cut into
    8 (1-inch) pieces
1 small onion, cut into 8
    wedges

4 (12-inch) metal skewers

Sauce

1 cup LAND O LAKES®
    Sour Cream
1/4 cup Italian dressing
1 tablespoon prepared
    horseradish

In large plastic food bag place sirloin pieces and $1/4$ cup Italian dressing; tightly seal bag. Turn bag several times to coat sirloin well. Place in 13x9-inch pan. Refrigerate at least 30 minutes.

Meanwhile, <u>prepare grill</u> placing coals to one side; heat until coals are ash white. Make aluminum foil drip pan; place opposite coals. In small bowl stir together all sauce ingredients; set aside.

To assemble kabobs on metal skewers alternately thread sirloin, mushrooms, tomatoes, green pepper and onion. Place kabobs on grill over drip pan. Grill, turning occasionally, until sirloin is desired doneness (10 to 15 minutes). Serve kabobs with sauce.
YIELD: 4 servings (1 cup sauce).

<u>Microwave Directions</u>: Use 6 (8-inch) wooden skewers. Prepare kabobs and sauce as directed above. Place kabobs in 12x8-inch baking dish. Cover; microwave on HIGH 5 minutes. Turn kabobs; microwave on HIGH until sirloin is desired doneness (4 to 5 minutes). Serve kabobs with sauce.

Nutrition Facts (1 serving): Calories 320; Protein 26g; Carbohydrate 14g; Fat 18g; Cholesterol 80mg; Sodium 240mg

Hamburgers *with* Cucumber Relish

*This relish, made with thinly sliced cucumber, tomatoes and red onion,
tastes great on grilled hamburgers.*

Preparation time: 30 minutes • Grilling time: 10 minutes

Hamburgers
$1^1/2$ pounds ground beef
$^1/4$ cup chopped onion
$^1/4$ teaspoon salt
$^1/4$ teaspoon pepper
2 tablespoons country-style
   Dijon mustard

Relish
1 teaspoon dill seed
1 teaspoon mustard seed
2 tablespoons cider vinegar
1 tablespoon vegetable oil
1 tablespoon country-style
   Dijon mustard
1 medium (1 cup) cucumber,
   thinly sliced
2 medium (1 cup) ripe
   tomatoes, thinly sliced
1 small (1 cup) red onion,
   thinly sliced, separated
   into rings

Prepare grill; heat until coals are ash white.

Meanwhile, in medium bowl stir together ground beef, onion, salt, pepper and 2 tablespoons mustard. Form into 6 large $^1/4$-inch thick patties; set aside.

In medium bowl combine all relish ingredients except cucumbers, tomatoes and onion. Add vegetables; toss to coat. Place hamburgers on grill. Grill, turning once, until desired doneness (10 to 15 minutes for medium). Spoon relish on hamburgers. **YIELD:** 6 servings.

Nutrition Facts (1 serving): Calories 270; Protein 19g; Carbohydrate 5g; Fat 19g; Cholesterol 70mg; Sodium 380mg

Grilled Stuffed Cheeseburger

Serve these cream cheese and olive-stuffed burgers with
Caesar salad and corn on the cob.

Preparation time: 30 minutes • Grilling time: 13 minutes

1 (3-ounce) package cream
  cheese, softened
1 (2^1/2-ounce) jar sliced
  mushrooms, drained
2 tablespoons chopped green
  pepper
^{1}/4 teaspoon garlic salt
^{1}/8 teaspoon pepper
2 pounds ground beef
4 ounces LAND O LAKES®
  Cheddar Cheese, cut into
  16 (2x1-inch) slices
4 Kaiser rolls, cut in half

<u>Prepare grill</u>; heat until coals are ash white.

Meanwhile, in small bowl stir together cream cheese, mushrooms, green pepper, garlic salt and pepper. Shape ground beef into 8 large ^{1}/2-inch thick patties. Place about <u>2 tablespoons</u> cream cheese mixture on top of each of <u>4</u> patties. Top each with remaining meat patty; press around edges to seal. Place hamburgers on grill. Grill, turning once, until desired doneness (12 to 15 minutes). Top each hamburger with <u>4 slices</u> cheese; continue grilling until cheese melts (1 minute). Serve hamburgers on rolls. **YIELD:** 4 sandwiches.

Nutrition Facts (1 sandwich): Calories 790; Protein 50g; Carbohydrate 32g; Fat 50g;
Cholesterol 190mg; Sodium 860mg

Spicy Jumbo Burger Olé

The addition of taco seasoning mix to the ground beef mixture gives this burger its spicy flavor.

Preparation time: 30 minutes • Chilling time: 30 minutes • Grilling time: 15 minutes

Hamburger
1/4 cup dry bread crumbs
1/4 cup finely chopped onion
1 1/2 pounds ground beef
1 egg, slightly beaten
1 (1 1/4-ounce) package taco
   seasoning mix

1 (7 to 8-inch) round unsliced
   loaf sourdough bread,
   sliced in half horizontally*
LAND O LAKES® Butter,
   softened

Toppings
4 LAND O LAKES® American
   Cheese Food Singles
Shredded lettuce
Chopped ripe tomato
Sliced pitted ripe olives
LAND O LAKES® Sour Cream
Guacamole
Salsa

Prepare grill; heat until coals are ash white.

Meanwhile, in large bowl combine all hamburger ingredients except bread and butter; mix well. Shape into 1 large (8 to 9-inch diameter) hamburger patty. Place on waxed paper lined cookie sheet; cover. Refrigerate at least 30 minutes.

Meanwhile, spread bread halves with butter; set aside.

Place hamburger on grill. Grill, turning once (if necessary, use two metal spatulas) until desired doneness (13 to 15 minutes).

Meanwhile, place bread halves, cut side down, alongside hamburger (not directly over coals). Grill bread, rotating occasionally, until toasted (3 to 4 minutes). Place 4 slices of cheese on hamburger; continue grilling until cheese is melted (2 to 4 minutes).

To serve, place hamburger on bottom bread half; top with lettuce, tomato, olives, sour cream, guacamole and salsa. Top with bread half. For easier serving, skewer with 6 skewers from top to bottom. Cut into 6 wedges. **YIELD**: 6 servings.

* If loaf of bread is too tall, slice into 3 horizontal layers. Remove center layer for other use.

TIP: If desired, jumbo burger can be made into 6 individual hamburgers and served on 6 hamburger buns. Shape hamburger mixture into 6 patties. Place hamburgers on grill. Grill, turning once, until desired doneness (12 to 15 minutes). Top with 1 slice cheese. Continue grilling until cheese is melted (about 1 minute). Toast buns and serve as directed above.

Nutrition Facts (1 serving): Calories 560; Protein 31g; Carbohydrate 50g; Fat 26g; Cholesterol 130mg; Sodium 1160mg

Western Barbecued Rib Sampler

Ribs are simmered in beer, then coated with a flavorful,
hot and spicy barbecue sauce.

Preparation time: 30 minutes • Cooking time: 45 minutes • Grilling time: 12 minutes

Ribs

- ¹/₂ cup firmly packed brown sugar
- ¹/₄ cup country-style Dijon mustard
- 2 (12-ounce) cans beer <u>or</u> non-alcoholic beer*
- 1 teaspoon hot pepper sauce
- 3 pounds country-style beef <u>or</u> pork ribs

Barbecue Sauce

- ¹/₄ cup firmly packed brown sugar
- ¹/₄ cup chopped onion
- 1 cup ketchup
- ¹/₂ cup Worcestershire sauce
- ¹/₄ cup lemon juice
- ¹/₂ teaspoon coarsely ground pepper
- ¹/₄ teaspoon ground red pepper
- ¹/₄ teaspoon salt

In Dutch oven stir together all rib ingredients <u>except</u> ribs; add ribs. Cook over high heat until mixture comes to a full boil (5 to 10 minutes). Cover; reduce heat to low. Continue cooking, turning ribs occasionally, until ribs are fork tender (40 to 50 minutes).

Meanwhile, <u>prepare grill</u>; heat until coals are ash white. In 1-quart saucepan stir together all barbecue sauce ingredients. Place ribs on grill. Brush ribs with barbecue sauce. Grill, brushing with barbecue sauce and turning occasionally, until ribs are fork tender and heated through (12 to 15 minutes). In 1-quart saucepan cook remaining barbecue sauce over medium heat, stirring occasionally, until just comes to a boil (3 to 5 minutes). Serve ribs with additional sauce. **YIELD:** 4 servings.

<u>Broiling Directions</u>: Prepare ribs as directed above. Do not grill. Heat broiler. Line broiler pan with aluminum foil; grease. Place ribs on prepared broiler pan 5 to 7 inches from heat. Brush with barbecue sauce. Broil, brushing with barbecue sauce and turning occasionally, until ribs are done (6 to 8 minutes). Cook remaining barbecue sauce over medium heat, stirring occasionally, until just comes to a boil (3 to 5 minutes). Serve with ribs.

*3 cups apple juice can be substituted for 2 (12-ounce) cans beer.

Nutrition Facts (1 serving): Calories 680; Protein 40g; Carbohydrate 70g; Fat 21g;
Cholesterol 115mg; Sodium 1750mg

Barbecue Pork Sandwiches

This barbecued shredded pork can be kept refrigerated and reheated in the microwave oven for a quick sandwich-on-the-run.

Preparation time: 15 minutes • Cooking time: 2 hours 21 minutes

Pork

2 pounds boneless pork shoulder roast

1 medium (1/2 cup) onion, chopped

2 teaspoons finely chopped fresh garlic

1/2 cup water

Sauce

1 (14-ounce) bottle (1 1/2 cups) ketchup

1 tablespoon chili powder

1 teaspoon firmly packed brown sugar

1/4 teaspoon coarsely ground pepper

1 tablespoon country-style Dijon mustard

3 tablespoons Worcestershire sauce

2 tablespoons cider vinegar

9 hamburger buns

Heat oven to 325°. In roasting pan place pork roast. Sprinkle with onion and garlic; add water. Cover; bake until roast shreds easily with fork (2 to 2 1/2 hours). Remove from pan. <u>Reserve pan juices</u>; skim off fat. With fork shred roast into small pieces.

In 3-quart saucepan combine all sauce ingredients and reserved pan juices. Cook over medium heat, stirring occasionally, until sauce comes to a full boil (6 to 8 minutes). Reduce heat to low; continue cooking 10 minutes. Stir in shredded pork. Continue cooking until heated through (5 to 8 minutes). **YIELD:** 9 sandwiches.

Nutrition Facts (1 sandwich): Calories 290; Protein 17g; Carbohydrate 36g; Fat 9g; Cholesterol 45mg; Sodium 850mg

Honey Mustard Glazed Ribs

Use a fresh orange for optimum flavor in the glaze.

Preparation time: 30 minutes • Cooking time: 20 minutes • Grilling time: 1 hour

Glaze

- 1 medium (¹/₂ cup) onion, chopped
- 2 tablespoons LAND O LAKES® Butter
- 1 cup honey
- ¹/₃ cup white wine vinegar
- 1 (8-ounce) jar country-style Dijon mustard
- ¹/₂ teaspoon salt
- ¹/₂ teaspoon grated orange peel
- 2 tablespoons orange juice

Ribs

- 4 pounds pork loin <u>or</u> spareribs

In 2-quart saucepan place onion and butter. Cook over medium heat, stirring occasionally, until onion is tender (6 to 8 minutes). Stir in all remaining glaze ingredients. Continue cooking, stirring occasionally, until mixture comes to a full boil (6 to 8 minutes). Turn heat to medium low; continue cooking until sauce thickens slightly and flavors blend (8 to 10 minutes). Remove from heat; <u>reserve ¹/₂ cup glaze</u>. Set aside remaining glaze.

Meanwhile, <u>prepare grill</u>; heat until coals are ash white. Make aluminum foil drip pan; place opposite coals. Place ribs on grill over drip pan. Cover; grill, turning once, until ribs are browned (40 to 50 minutes). Brush tops of ribs with <u>¹/₄ cup</u> reserved glaze; continue grilling for 10 to 15 minutes. Turn ribs; brush with remaining ¹/₄ cup reserved glaze. Continue grilling until ribs are fork tender (10 to 15 minutes). Serve with remaining glaze. **YIELD:** 6 servings (2 cups glaze).

TIP: Glaze can also be used on chicken, pork or beef.

Nutrition Facts (1 serving): Calories 710; Protein 36g; Carbohydrate 51g; Fat 41g; Cholesterol 155mg; Sodium 800mg

Pork Chops *with* Green Peppercorn Sauce

Peppercorns were sometimes used as currency in Europe during the fifteenth century since they were so rare.

Preparation time: 45 minutes • Grilling time: 8 minutes

Sauce

1 cup sliced fresh mushrooms
1/3 cup chopped onion
1/4 cup LAND O LAKES®
    Butter
1/2 cup dry white wine <u>or</u>
    chicken broth
1/3 cup chicken broth
1/4 cup chopped fresh parsley
1 cup LAND O LAKES®
    Sour Cream
2 to 4 teaspoons green
    peppercorns in brine, well
    drained
2 teaspoons country-style
    Dijon mustard

Chops

1 tablespoon olive <u>or</u>
    vegetable oil
6 (3/4-inch thick) pork chops
Coarsely ground pepper

<u>Prepare grill</u>; heat until coals are ash white.

Meanwhile, in 2-quart saucepan stir together mushrooms, onion and butter. Cook over medium heat, stirring occasionally, until mushrooms and onion are tender (8 to 10 minutes). Stir in white wine and chicken broth. Continue cooking, stirring occasionally, until liquid is reduced to about 2 tablespoons (20 to 30 minutes). Stir in parsley, sour cream, peppercorns and mustard. Continue cooking until heated through (5 to 8 minutes).

Meanwhile, brush $1/4$ teaspoon oil on both sides of each pork chop; sprinkle with pepper. Place chops on grill. Cover; grill, turning once, until desired doneness (8 to 10 minutes). Serve chops with peppercorn sauce. **YIELD**: 6 servings ($1^1/4$ cups sauce).

Nutrition Facts (1 serving): Calories 340; Protein 27g; Carbohydrate 6g; Fat 21g; Cholesterol 100mg; Sodium 240mg

Pork Roast *with* Rhubarb Chutney

Fruit chutney is delicious served with roasted pork.

Preparation time: 30 minutes • Grilling time: 1 hour 30 minutes • Cooking time: 1 hour

Roast

- 1 tablespoon chopped fresh rosemary*
- 1/2 teaspoon salt
- 1/4 teaspoon coarsely ground pepper
- 1 (2 1/2-pound) boneless pork loin roast

Chutney

- 2 cups fresh <u>or</u> frozen red raspberries
- 2 cups fresh <u>or</u> frozen sliced rhubarb
- 1 stalk (1/2 cup) celery, sliced
- 1 medium (1/2 cup) onion, chopped
- 1/2 cup golden raisins
- 1 cup honey
- 1/3 cup raspberry vinegar <u>or</u> white vinegar
- 1 tablespoon chopped fresh gingerroot**
- 1/2 teaspoon cinnamon
- 1/4 teaspoon dry mustard
- 1/8 teaspoon ground cloves

<u>Prepare grill</u> placing coals to one side; heat until coals are ash white. Make aluminum foil drip pan; place opposite coals. In small bowl stir together rosemary, salt and pepper. Rub mixture all over surface of pork roast. Place roast on grill over drip pan. Cover; grill, turning once, until meat thermometer reaches 160°F (Medium) or desired doneness (1 1/2 to 2 hours). Slice into 1/2-inch slices.

Meanwhile, in 3-quart saucepan combine all chutney ingredients. Cook over medium heat, stirring occasionally, until chutney comes to a full boil (10 to 12 minutes). Reduce heat to low; continue cooking until chutney thickens (about 1 to 1 1/2 hours). Remove from heat. Serve pork slices with chutney. **YIELD:** 10 servings (3 cups chutney).

*1 teaspoon dried rosemary can be substituted for 1 tablespoon chopped fresh rosemary.

** 3/4 teaspoon ground ginger can be substituted for 1 tablespoon chopped fresh gingerroot.

Nutrition Facts (1 serving): Calories 340; Protein 27g; Carbohydrate 39g; Fat 9g; Cholesterol 70mg; Sodium 170mg

Mint Pesto Lamb Chops

*Pesto is made with fresh mint and walnuts, then served
with lamb chops and grilled tomatoes.*

Preparation time: 30 minutes • Grilling time: 12 minutes

Pesto
- $1/2$ cup chopped walnuts
- $1/2$ cup chopped fresh mint leaves
- $1/3$ cup olive <u>or</u> vegetable oil
- 2 tablespoons freshly grated Parmesan cheese
- $1/4$ teaspoon coarsely ground pepper
- 1 teaspoon finely chopped fresh garlic

Lamb Chops
- $1/8$ teaspoon salt
- $1/8$ teaspoon coarsely ground pepper
- 2 tablespoons olive <u>or</u> vegetable oil
- 6 (1-inch thick) lamb loin chops
- 3 ripe tomatoes, halved
- 2 tablespoons freshly grated Parmesan cheese

<u>Prepare grill</u>; heat until coals are ash white. In medium bowl stir together all pesto ingredients; set aside.

In small bowl stir together salt, $1/8$ teaspoon pepper and 2 tablespoons oil. Brush lamb chops with oil mixture; place on grill. Grill, basting and turning occasionally, until fork tender (10 to 15 minutes). Spoon about <u>1 tablespoon</u> pesto on each lamb chop. Place tomato halves on grill; spoon about <u>1 teaspoon</u> Parmesan cheese on each tomato half. Continue grilling until heated through (2 to 4 minutes). Serve tomato half alongside each lamb chop; serve with remaining pesto.
YIELD: 6 servings ($3/4$ cup pesto).

<u>Broiler Directions</u>: Prepare pesto and lamb chops as directed above; place on broiler pan. Broil 3 to 5 inches from heat, turning once, until fork tender (10 to 15 minutes). Spoon <u>1 tablespoon</u> pesto on each lamb chop. Place tomato halves on broiler pan; spoon about <u>1 teaspoon</u> Parmesan cheese on each tomato half. Continue broiling until heated through (2 to 4 minutes). Serve tomato half alongside each lamb chop; serve with remaining pesto.

*Nutrition Facts (1 serving): Calories 260; Protein 22g; Carbohydrate 5g; Fat 29g;
Cholesterol 70mg; Sodium 170mg*

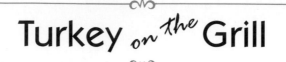

Turkey on the Grill

Juicy, tender turkey, cooked outdoors, is the center of a perfect summer meal.

Preparation time: 30 minutes • Grilling time: 3 hours

<u>Kettle or Covered Grill</u>: Thaw and prepare 10 to 12-pound turkey for roasting as directed on package; do not stuff. Season cavity with salt and brush skin with melted LAND O LAKES® Butter. <u>Prepare grill</u> placing coals to one side; heat until coals are ash white. Make aluminum foil drip pan; place opposite coals. Place top grilling rack over coals and drip pan. Place prepared turkey on grill over drip pan. Open bottom vents directly under coals. Cover grill, positioning top vent directly over side of grill with turkey. Adjust vent as necessary to keep a consistently hot fire. Add coals to fire as necessary. Grill turkey 11 to 20 minutes per pound, turning halfway through the time and basting with LAND O LAKES® Butter. Turkey is done when thermometer inserted into thigh muscle reaches 180 to 185°F.

<u>Gas Grill</u>: Thaw and prepare 10 to 12-pound turkey for roasting as directed on package; do not stuff. Season cavity with salt and brush skin with melted LAND O LAKES® Butter. If dual control gas grill is used, make aluminum foil drip pan; place over coals on one side of grill, then heat other side 10 to 15 minutes on high. If single control gas grill is used, make aluminum foil drip pan; place over one half of coals to block out direct heat, then heat grill 10 to 15 minutes on high. Reduce heat to medium. Replace top rack; place turkey on rack directly above drip pan. Grill turkey on medium heat 11 to 20 minutes per pound, turning halfway through the time and basting with LAND O LAKES® Butter. Turkey is done when thermometer inserted into thigh muscle reaches 180 to 185°F.

Nutrition Facts (3 ounces cooked turkey): Calories 140; Protein 25g; Carbohydrate 0g; Fat 4g; Cholesterol 65mg; Sodium 60mg

Herbed Hickory-Smoked Cornish Hens

Hickory chips are widely used to add flavor to grilled turkey or ham.

Preparation time: 30 minutes • Grilling time: 1 hour 10 minutes

2¹/₂ cups hickory chips

6 tablespoons LAND O LAKES® Butter, melted

2 tablespoons dry sherry, if desired

1 tablespoon chopped fresh sage leaves*

1 tablespoon chopped fresh rosemary**

1 (16-ounce) bag frozen small whole onions, thawed

4 Cornish game hens, thawed, giblets removed

2 cloves garlic, cut in half

16 whole sage leaves***

In medium bowl cover hickory chips with water; soak 30 minutes. Prepare grill placing coals to one side; heat until coals are ash white. Make aluminum foil drip pan; place opposite coals. In medium bowl stir together butter, sherry, 1 tablespoon sage and rosemary; reserve 3 tablespoons mixture for basting game hens. Stir onions into remaining butter mixture; set aside.

Rub skin of game hens with cut garlic; place piece of garlic in cavity of each game hen. Loosen skin over breast of each game hen; place 4 sage leaves under skin. Spoon ¹/₄ onion mixture into each game hen; secure opening with metal skewers. Tie legs together. Place game hens on grill over drip pan. Baste with reserved herb butter. Grill 40 minutes; turn and baste. Continue grilling until fork tender (30 to 40 minutes). **YIELD:** 4 servings.

* 1 teaspoon dried sage leaves can be substituted for 1 tablespoon chopped fresh sage leaves.

** 1 teaspoon dried rosemary can be substituted for 1 tablespoon chopped fresh rosemary.

***1 tablespoon dried sage leaves can be substituted for 16 whole sage leaves.

Nutrition Facts (1 serving): Calories 200; Protein 25g; Carbohydrate 0g; Fat 11g; Cholesterol 85mg; Sodium 115mg

Tangy Grilled Chicken

This tangy sauce, slightly spicy, is excellent on chicken, beef and ribs.

Preparation time: 20 minutes • Cooking time: 1 hour • Grilling time: 40 minutes

Sauce

- 2 tablespoons LAND O LAKES® Butter
- 1/4 cup finely chopped onion
- 2 teaspoons finely chopped fresh garlic
- 1 (14 1/2-ounce) can whole tomatoes, coarsely chopped, reserve juice
- 1/4 cup Worcestershire sauce
- 1/4 cup pineapple juice
- 2 tablespoons firmly packed brown sugar
- 1 teaspoon crushed red pepper flakes
- 2 tablespoons cider vinegar
- 2 tablespoons molasses
- 1/4 teaspoon liquid smoke

Chicken

- 1 (3 to 4-pound) frying chicken, cut into 8 pieces

In 2-quart saucepan melt butter over medium heat. Add onion and garlic; continue cooking until onion is crisply tender (1 to 2 minutes). Add tomatoes and reserved juice. Stir in all remaining sauce ingredients. Reduce heat to low; continue cooking 1 hour. Reserve 1 cup sauce; set aside remaining 1 cup sauce.

Meanwhile, prepare grill placing coals to one side; heat until coals are ash white. Make aluminum foil drip pan; place opposite coals. Place chicken on grill over drip pan. Grill, turning occasionally, 25 minutes. Continue grilling, basting occasionally with reserved 1 cup sauce, until chicken is fork tender (15 to 20 minutes). Serve chicken with remaining 1 cup sauce. **YIELD:** 6 servings (2 cups sauce).

Nutrition Facts (1 serving): Calories 200; Protein 28g; Carbohydrate 4g; Fat 8g; Cholesterol 85mg; Sodium 150mg

Caribbean Chicken *with* Mango Chutney

Caribbean cooking is known for its "jerk" chicken, an intriguing dish that features chicken coated with a mixture of highly flavorful spices.

Preparation time: 25 minutes • Marinating time: 4 hours • Broiling time: 35 minutes

Marinade

- 1/2 cup orange juice
- 1/4 cup vegetable oil
- 1 tablespoon chopped fresh basil leaves*
- 1 tablespoon chopped fresh oregano leaves**
- 1 tablespoon country-style Dijon mustard
- 1 teaspoon finely chopped fresh garlic
- 2 tablespoons lime juice

Chicken

- 4 (about 7 ounces each) chicken thighs with legs attached

Chutney

- 1 large (1 1/2 cups) mango, peeled, chopped
- 1/4 cup chopped red onion
- 1/4 cup tarragon vinegar
- 1/4 cup lime juice
- 1 tablespoon honey
- 2 teaspoons finely chopped fresh gingerroot***
- 2 teaspoons chopped fresh mint leaves

In large plastic food bag combine all marinade ingredients; add chicken thighs. Tightly seal bag. Turn bag several times to coat chicken. Place in 13x9-inch pan. Refrigerate, turning occasionally, at least 4 hours or overnight. Meanwhile, in medium bowl combine all chutney ingredients. Cover; refrigerate at least 4 hours or overnight. Remove chicken from marinade. In 1-quart saucepan bring marinade to a full boil. Remove chutney from refrigerator; let stand at room temperature 30 minutes. Meanwhile, heat broiler. Place chicken on greased broiler pan. Broil 6 to 8 inches from heat, turning every 10 minutes and basting with marinade, until chicken is fork tender (30 to 35 minutes). Serve chutney with chicken. **YIELD:** 4 servings.

Grilling Directions: Prepare grill placing coals to one side; heat until coals are ash white. Make aluminum foil drip pan; place opposite coals. Place chicken on grill over drip pan. Grill, turning and basting occasionally with marinade, until chicken is fork tender (40 to 50 minutes).

* 1 teaspoon dried basil leaves can be substituted for 1 tablespoon chopped fresh basil leaves.

** 1 teaspoon dried oregano leaves can be substituted for 1 tablespoon chopped fresh oregano leaves.

*** 3/4 teaspoon ground ginger can be substituted for 2 teaspoons finely chopped fresh gingerroot.

Nutrition Information (1 serving): Calories 320; Protein 27g; Carbohydrate 20g; Fat 15g; Cholesterol 90mg; Sodium 120mg

Spiced-Cherry Chicken

*The sweetness of the cherry preserves complements
the hotness of the dry spice rub in this recipe.*

Preparation time: 10 minutes • Broiling time: 22 minutes • Cooking time: 8 minutes

Spice Rub

  2 teaspoons garlic powder

  2 teaspoons onion salt

1¹/₂ teaspoons dried marjoram leaves

1¹/₂ teaspoons dry mustard

1¹/₂ teaspoon paprika

  1 teaspoon chili powder

¹/₄ teaspoon ground cloves

Chicken

16 chicken wings

Sauce

  1 (10-ounce) jar cherry preserves

¹/₂ cup orange juice

  6 tablespoons dry sherry <u>or</u> orange juice

  4 teaspoons cornstarch

In small bowl combine all spice rub ingredients; rub onto chicken wings. <u>Heat broiler</u>. Place chicken on greased broiler pan. Broil 6 to 8 inches from heat, turning every 5 minutes, until chicken is fork tender (16 to 22 minutes). Meanwhile, in 1-quart saucepan combine all sauce ingredients. Cook over medium heat, stirring often, until thickened (6 to 8 minutes). Serve sauce over chicken.
YIELD: 4 servings.

<u>Grilling Directions</u>: Prepare grill placing coals to one side; heat until coals are ash white. Make aluminum foil drip pan; place opposite coals. Place chicken on grill over drip pan. Grill, turning occasionally, until chicken is fork tender (30 to 35 minutes).

Nutrition Information (1 serving): Calories 660; Protein 38g; Carbohydrate 60g; Fat 27g; Cholesterol 110mg; Sodium 980mg

Quick Chicken Southwest

Salsa, avocado and cheese bring southwestern flavors to this grilled chicken.

Preparation time: 30 minutes • Marinating time: 4 hours • Grilling time: 13 minutes

Marinade

- ¼ cup lime juice
- ¼ cup vegetable oil
- 2 tablespoons chopped fresh cilantro or parsley
- 1 teaspoon finely chopped fresh garlic

- 2 (12 ounces each) whole boneless chicken breasts, skinned, halved

Toppings

- 8 slices (2¼x1x⅛-inch) LAND O LAKES® Cheddar or Monterey Jack Cheese
- 3 cups hot cooked rice
- 1 cup thick salsa, heated
- 8 avocado slices

In large plastic food bag combine all marinade ingredients <u>except</u> chicken breasts; add chicken. Tightly seal bag. Turn bag several times to coat chicken. Place in 13x9-inch pan. Refrigerate at least 4 hours or overnight. <u>Prepare grill</u>; heat until coals are ash white. Remove chicken from marinade; drain. Place chicken on grill. Grill 5 minutes; turn. Continue grilling until chicken is fork tender (4 to 6 minutes). Top each chicken breast with <u>2 slices</u> cheese. Continue grilling until cheese begins to melt (1 to 2 minutes). Line serving platter with rice. Top rice with chicken breasts, warm salsa and avocado slices.

YIELD: 4 servings.

Nutrition Information (1 serving): Calories 580; Protein 36g; Carbohydrate 52g; Fat 24g; Cholesterol 95mg; Sodium 700mg

Glazed Chicken & Orange Salsa

This simple orange salsa is also delicious served with fish.

Preparation time: 30 minutes • Chilling time: 1 hour • Grilling time: 10 minutes

Orange Salsa

- 2 medium (1 cup) seedless oranges, segmented, membrane removed, chopped
- 1 tablespoon sugar
- 2 tablespoons sliced green onion
- 2 tablespoons chopped fresh parsley

Chicken

- 2 (12 ounces each) whole boneless chicken breasts, skinned, halved
- 1/2 teaspoon salt
- 1/8 teaspoon pepper

Glaze

- 3 tablespoons LAND O LAKES® Butter, melted
- 1 cup orange juice
- 1 tablespoon cornstarch

In small bowl stir together all orange salsa ingredients; refrigerate at least 1 hour.

Meanwhile, prepare grill; heat until coals are ash white. Sprinkle chicken breasts with salt and pepper.

In 1-quart saucepan stir together all glaze ingredients. Cook over medium heat, stirring constantly, until mixture thickens and comes to a full boil (5 to 7 minutes). Place chicken on grill; brush with glaze. Grill, turning once and brushing with glaze, until chicken is fork tender (10 to 12 minutes). Serve chicken with orange salsa.
YIELD: 4 servings ($3/4$ cup salsa).

Nutrition Facts (1 serving): Calories 190; Protein 25g; Carbohydrate 11g; Fat 5g; Cholesterol 70mg; Sodium 350mg

Chicken Breasts Southwestern

*Green chilies and salsa add south-of-the-border flavor
to grilled chicken breasts.*

Preparation time: 15 minutes • Grilling time: 14 minutes

Marinade

- 2/3 cup vegetable oil
- 1/3 cup lime juice
- 2 tablespoons chopped green chilies
- 1 teaspoon finely chopped fresh garlic

Chicken

- 2 (12 ounces each) whole boneless chicken breasts, skinned, halved
- 8 (2x1x1/4-inch) slices LAND O LAKES® Cheddar Cheese

  Salsa

In large plastic food bag place all marinade ingredients; add chicken breasts. Tightly seal bag. Turn bag several times to coat chicken well. Place in 13x9-inch pan. Refrigerate at least 45 minutes.

Meanwhile, <u>prepare grill</u> placing coals to one side; heat until coals are ash white. Make aluminum foil drip pan; place opposite coals. Place chicken on grill over drip pan. Grill chicken, turning once, until fork tender (13 to 15 minutes). Top each chicken breast with 2 slices cheese. Continue grilling until cheese begins to melt (1 to 2 minutes). Serve with salsa. **YIELD:** 4 servings.

*Nutrition Facts (1 serving): Calories 280; Protein 30g; Carbohydrate 1g; Fat 17g;
Cholesterol 90mg; Sodium 170mg*

Barbecued Chicken Bundles

These tasty bundles can be assembled ahead of time,
covered and refrigerated before grilling.

Preparation time: 30 minutes • Grilling time: 40 minutes

4 (12 ounces each) whole
   boneless chicken breasts,
   skinned, halved

8 (1x1x½-inch)
   chunks (4 ounces)
   LAND O LAKES®
   Cheddar Cheese

16 (about ¾ pound)
   slices bacon

¼ cup barbecue sauce

Prepare grill placing coals to one side; heat until coals are ash white. Make aluminum foil drip pan; place opposite coals. Make slit in each chicken breast half to form pocket. Place <u>1 chunk</u> cheese in each pocket. Roll each chicken breast into bundle and wrap crisscross with <u>2 slices</u> bacon. Secure bacon with toothpicks. Place bundles on grill over drip pan. Grill, turning every 15 minutes and brushing with barbecue sauce during last 10 minutes, until chicken is fork tender (30 to 40 minutes). If crisp bacon is desired, place bundles over direct heat, turning 2 to 3 times, during last 10 minutes. **YIELD:** 8 servings.

<u>Oven Directions</u>: Heat oven to 400°. Prepare bundles as directed above (if crisp bacon is desired, precook bacon until half done). Place bundles, bottom-side up, on broiler pan. Bake for 30 minutes; turn. Brush with barbecue sauce. Continue baking for 20 to 30 minutes or until chicken is fork tender.

Nutrition Information (1 serving): Calories 280; Protein 34g; Carbohydrate 1g; Fat 15g;
Cholesterol 100mg; Sodium 430mg

Teriyaki Chicken Kabobs

The brown sugar in this marinade gives these kabobs a light glaze.

Preparation time: 30 minutes • Marinating time: 3 hours • Grilling time: 15 minutes

Marinade

- $1/3$ cup lemon juice
- $1/4$ cup LAND O LAKES® Butter, melted
- $1/4$ cup soy sauce
- 2 tablespoons firmly packed brown sugar
- $1/2$ teaspoon ground ginger
- $1/4$ teaspoon pepper
- 3 tablespoons ketchup
- 1 teaspoon finely chopped fresh garlic

Chicken

- 1 pound boneless chicken breast, cut into about 32 (1-inch) pieces

Kabobs

- 8 (1-inch) pineapple chunks
- 8 cherry tomatoes
- 1 small green pepper, cut into 8 (1-inch) pieces
- 1 small zucchini, cut into 8 (1-inch) pieces

- 4 (12-inch) metal skewers

  Hot cooked wild rice

In large plastic food bag combine all marinade ingredients; add chicken pieces. Tightly seal bag. Turn bag several times to coat chicken well. Place in 13x9-inch pan. Refrigerate, turning occasionally, at least 3 hours. Drain; <u>reserve marinade</u>.

<u>Prepare grill</u> placing coals to one side; heat until coals are ash white. Make aluminum foil drip pan; place opposite coals. To assemble kabobs on metal skewers alternately thread chicken, pineapple, tomatoes, green pepper and zucchini. Brush kabobs with marinade. Place kabobs on grill over drip pan. Grill, turning and basting with marinade occasionally, until chicken is fork tender (15 to 20 minutes). Serve with wild rice. **YIELD:** 4 servings.

Nutrition Facts (1 serving without rice): Calories 240; Protein 26g; Carbohydrate 15g; Fat 9g; Cholesterol 80mg; Sodium 720mg

Chicken Vinaigrette Salad

The tangy mustard dressing would also be delicious on cold beef salads.

Preparation time: 30 minutes • Marinating time: 30 minutes • Grilling time: 10 minutes • Chilling time: 2 hours

Dressing

¹/₂ cup vegetable oil

2 tablespoons white wine vinegar

1 tablespoon stone ground prepared mustard

1 tablespoon honey

Salad

2 (12 ounces each) whole boneless chicken breasts, skinned, halved

1 pound fresh spinach, washed, trimmed, torn into bite-size pieces

6 to 8 radishes, sliced

4 ounces LAND O LAKES® Swiss Cheese, cut into julienne strips

In jar with tight-fitting lid combine all dressing ingredients; shake well. Place chicken breast halves in large plastic food bag; add ¹/₄ cup dressing. Tightly seal bag. Turn bag several times to coat chicken well. Place in 13x9-inch pan. Refrigerate at least 30 minutes.

Meanwhile, prepare grill; heat until coals are ash white. Place chicken on grill. Grill, turning once, until chicken is fork tender (10 to 12 minutes). Remove from grill. Cover; refrigerate at least 2 hours or until chilled.

Just before serving, in large bowl toss together spinach, radishes and cheese. Portion onto 4 individual plates. Slice chilled chicken breasts diagonally; place one sliced chicken breast on top of each salad. Serve with dressing. **YIELD:** 4 servings.

Nutrition Facts (1 serving): Calories 460; Protein 38g; Carbohydrate 9g; Fat 30g; Cholesterol 100mg; Sodium 260mg

Grilled Oriental Chicken Pasta Salad

*Grilled chicken breasts top a mixture of Oriental
vegetables and noodles.*

Preparation time: 40 minutes • Grilling time: 18 minutes

Chicken

2 (12 ounces each) whole
    boneless chicken breasts,
    skinned, halved
2 tablespoons soy sauce
2 (3-ounce) packages Oriental
    flavor ramen noodle soup

Dressing

1/3 cup vegetable oil
1/3 cup rice vinegar or white
    wine vinegar
1 seasoning packet from soup
    mix
3/4 teaspoon ginger
3/4 teaspoon finely chopped
    fresh garlic

Salad

1 cup pea pods, remove tips
    and strings, cut in half
1/2 cup chopped green onions
2 medium (1 cup) carrots, cut
    into very thin 2-inch
    julienne strips
1/4 cup salted cashews

Prepare grill placing coals to one side; heat until coals are ash white.
Make aluminum foil drip pan; place opposite coals. Brush chicken
with soy sauce. Place chicken on grill over drip pan. Grill, turning
chicken over after half the time, until chicken is fork tender (14 to
18 minutes). Meanwhile, in 2-quart saucepan cook both packages of
noodle soup according to package directions <u>using only 1 seasoning
packet</u>; drain. Meanwhile, in jar with tight fitting lid, combine all
dressing ingredients; shake well. In large bowl toss together noodles
and all salad ingredients <u>except</u> cashews; toss gently with dressing.
Slice each chicken breast half crosswise into 1-inch pieces; do not
separate. To serve, divide salad among 4 plates. Place one chicken
breast half on top of each salad. Sprinkle with cashews.
YIELD: 4 servings.

*Nutrition Information (1 serving): Calories 580; Protein 35g; Carbohydrate 37g; Fat 32g;
Cholesterol 85mg; Sodium 1480mg.*

Shrimp & Artichoke Kabobs

*Shrimp and marinated artichoke kabobs are
served over a lemon-zested pasta.*

Preparation time: 40 minutes • Grilling time: 10 minutes

9 ounces uncooked fresh
  linguini*

1 pound (about 24 medium)
  fresh <u>or</u> frozen raw shrimp

1 medium red onion, cut into
  12 wedges

2 (6-ounce) jars marinated
  artichokes, <u>reserve marinade</u>

6 (12-inch) metal skewers

Basting Sauce

2 teaspoons dried basil leaves

1/2 teaspoon salt

1/2 teaspoon coarsely ground
  pepper

Dash ground red pepper

1/2 teaspoon finely chopped
  fresh garlic

2 tablespoons olive <u>or</u>
  vegetable oil

2 teaspoons grated lemon
  peel

Prepare grill; heat until coals are ash white. Cook linguini according to package directions. Rinse with hot water; drain. Place in large bowl; set aside. Meanwhile, peel and devein shrimp, leaving tail intact. (If shrimp are frozen, do not thaw; peel under running cold water.) Alternate shrimp, onion and artichokes on skewers. In small bowl stir together 2 tablespoons reserved marinade and all basting sauce ingredients <u>except</u> lemon peel; brush over kabobs. Place kabobs on grill. Grill, basting and turning occasionally, for 7 to 10 minutes or until shrimp turn pink. Meanwhile, add remaining artichoke marinade and lemon peel to linguini; toss to coat. Serve kabobs with hot cooked linguini. **YIELD:** 6 servings.

* 9 ounces uncooked dried linguini can be substituted for 9 ounces uncooked fresh linguini.

Nutrition Information (1 serving): Calories 300; Protein 18g; Carbohydrate 40g; Fat 8g; Cholesterol 85mg; Sodium 240mg.

Fish Steaks *with* Sweet Red Pepper Puree

Serve these special grilled fish steaks when entertaining friends.

Preparation time: 15 minutes • Marinating time: 2 hours • Broiling time: 5 minutes • Cooking time: 26 minutes • Grilling time: 8 minutes

Marinade
- 1/3 cup lemon juice
- 1/4 cup olive <u>or</u> vegetable oil
- 1 tablespoon chopped fresh thyme leaves*
- 1/2 teaspoon salt

- 1 1/2 pounds fish steaks (halibut, grouper, amberjack, swordfish, etc.)

Red Pepper Sauce
- 1 red pepper, cut in half, seeded
- 1/3 cup dry white wine <u>or</u> unsweetened white grape juice
- 2 tablespoons chopped green onions
- 1/2 cup whipping cream

In small bowl stir together all marinade ingredients. Place fish steaks in 8-inch glass baking dish; pour marinade over fish. Cover with plastic food wrap; refrigerate 2 hours.

Meanwhile, place red pepper halves, cut side down, on broiler pan. Broil 4 to 6 inches from heat until skin blackens (5 to 10 minutes). Wrap in damp paper towels; place in plastic food bag. Let stand 10 minutes.

Peel skins from peppers; discard skin. In 5-cup blender container place peppers. Cover; blend at high until smooth (30 to 45 seconds). Pour into 1-quart saucepan. Stir in white wine and green onions. Cook over medium heat, stirring occasionally, until sauce comes to a full boil (6 to 8 minutes). Reduce heat to low; continue cooking, stirring occasionally, until flavors blend and sauce thickens slightly (12 to 15 minutes). Stir in whipping cream. Continue cooking until sauce is heated through (8 to 10 minutes).

Meanwhile, <u>prepare grill</u>; heat until coals are ash white. Place fish on grill. Cover; grill, turning once, until fish flakes with a fork (8 to 10 minutes). On each serving plate place about <u>3 tablespoons</u> red pepper sauce; top with fish. **YIELD:** 4 servings (1 cup sauce).

* 1 teaspoon dried thyme leaves can be substituted for 1 tablespoon chopped fresh thyme leaves.

Nutrition Facts (1 serving): Calories 290; Protein 29g; Carbohydrate 3g; Fat 16g; Cholesterol 95mg; Sodium 160mg

Swordfish *with* Peach Pepper Salsa

This spicy peach salsa would also taste great with grilled chicken or pork.

Preparation time: 30 minutes • Standing time: 1 hour • Grilling time: 8 minutes

Salsa

  2 large (2 cups) ripe peaches, coarsely chopped (fresh <u>or</u> frozen)

  1 cup chopped assorted peppers (red, yellow, orange <u>or</u> green)

$^1\!/_4$ cup chopped fresh cilantro

$^1\!/_4$ cup chopped red onion

$^1\!/_2$ teaspoon ground cumin

$^1\!/_2$ teaspoon coarsely ground pepper

  1 teaspoon finely chopped seeded jalapeño pepper

  1 teaspoon grated lime peel

  3 tablespoons olive <u>or</u> vegetable oil

  1 tablespoon lime juice

Swordfish

  2 pounds swordfish steaks, cut into 6 pieces

     Olive <u>or</u> vegetable oil

In medium bowl stir together all salsa ingredients. Cover; set aside for 1 to 2 hours to blend flavors.

Meanwhile, <u>prepare grill</u>; heat until coals are ash white. Brush swordfish with oil; place on grill. Cover; grill, turning once, until swordfish flakes with a fork (8 to 10 minutes). Serve swordfish with salsa.

YIELD: 6 servings (2 cups salsa).

Nutrition Facts (1 serving): Calories 270; Protein 26g; Carbohydrate 8g; Fat 14g; Cholesterol 50mg; Sodium 115mg

Grilled Salmon *with* Tarragon Butter

Tarragon is an aromatic herb with a distinct aniselike flavor.

Preparation time: 30 minutes • Grilling time: 10 minutes

1/2 cup LAND O LAKES®
     Butter, softened
  1 tablespoon chopped fresh
     tarragon leaves*
  1 teaspoon lemon juice

  4 (1-inch thick) salmon steaks

<u>Prepare grill</u> placing coals to one side; heat until coals are ash white. Make aluminum foil drip pan; place opposite coals.

Meanwhile, in small bowl stir together butter, tarragon and lemon juice. Divide butter mixture in half; reserve half. Spread <u>1 teaspoon</u> butter mixture on both sides of each salmon steak. Grill, turning once, until salmon flakes with a fork (10 to 12 minutes). Serve salmon with reserved butter mixture. **YIELD:** 4 servings.

* 1 teaspoon dried tarragon leaves can be substituted for 1 tablespoon chopped fresh tarragon leaves.

Nutrition Facts (1 serving): Calories 340; Protein 19g; Carbohydrate 0g; Fat 29g; Cholesterol 115mg; Sodium 280mg

Rainbow Trout *with* Crunchy Gazpacho

This chunky cold tomato and vegetable sauce, ladled over rainbow trout, presents glorious color and flavor.

Preparation time: 25 minutes • Cooking time: 8 minutes

Gazpacho

- 2 medium (2 cups) ripe tomatoes, cut into $1/2$-inch pieces
- 1 medium (1 cup) cucumber, peeled, cut into $1/2$-inch pieces
- 1 medium (1 cup) red <u>or</u> green pepper, cut into $1/2$-inch pieces
- 1 cup red onion, cut into $1/4$-inch pieces
- $1/4$ cup chopped fresh parsley
- $1/4$ cup olive <u>or</u> vegetable oil
- $1/2$ teaspoon salt
- $1/2$ teaspoon pepper
- 3 tablespoons red wine vinegar
- 1 tablespoon Worcestershire sauce
- $1/4$ teaspoon hot pepper sauce

Trout

- $1/4$ cup LAND O LAKES® Butter
- $1/2$ teaspoon finely chopped fresh garlic
- $1/2$ cup chopped red onion
- $1/4$ cup chopped fresh parsley
- $1/2$ teaspoon salt
- $1/4$ teaspoon pepper
- 6 ($1/2$ to $3/4$-pound) pan-dressed rainbow trout

In medium bowl stir together all gazpacho ingredients. In 5-cup blender container place about <u>2 cups</u> mixture. Cover; blend on high speed until saucy (30 to 45 seconds). Stir back into remaining gazpacho mixture; set aside.

In 10-inch skillet melt butter and garlic until sizzling. In small bowl stir together all remaining trout ingredients <u>except</u> trout. Place about <u>2 tablespoons</u> mixture in cavity of each trout. Place 3 trout in skillet; cook over medium high heat, turning once, until fish flakes with a fork (8 to 10 minutes). Remove to serving platter; keep warm. Repeat with remaining trout. Spoon 1 cup sauce over trout; serve remaining sauce with trout. **YIELD:** 6 servings.

<u>Grilling Directions</u>: Omit butter and garlic. Prepare gazpacho as directed above. <u>Prepare grill</u>; heat until coals are ash white. Prepare trout as directed above. Brush trout with vegetable oil. Grill trout over medium hot coals, turning once, until fish flakes with a fork (14 to 20 minutes). Remove to serving platter. Spoon 1 cup sauce over trout; serve remaining sauce with trout.

Nutrition Facts (1 serving): Calories 420; Protein 34g; Carbohydrate 9g; Fat 27g; Cholesterol 110mg; Sodium 550mg

easy Side Dishes!

Old-World Potato Salad
and Crunchy Cabbage Salad

Old-World Potato Salad

Carrot slices, green pepper and sour cream add a touch of difference to this creamy potato salad.

Preparation time: 30 minutes • Chilling time: 3 hours (pictured on page 200)

2 pounds (3 to 5 medium) russet potatoes, cooked, peeled, sliced
3/4 cup sliced 1/4-inch carrots
1/2 cup chopped green pepper

1 1/2 cups LAND O LAKES® Sour Cream
1 tablespoon sugar
1 teaspoon salt
1/2 teaspoon dried dill weed
1/4 teaspoon pepper
2 teaspoons prepared mustard
2 tablespoons vinegar

Chopped fresh dill, if desired

In large bowl combine potatoes, carrots and green pepper. In medium bowl stir together all remaining ingredients <u>except</u> fresh dill. Add to potato mixture; stir to coat well. Refrigerate at least 3 hours. Sprinkle with dill, if desired. **YIELD:** 6 servings.

Nutrition Information (1 serving): Calories 210; Protein 6g; Carbohydrate 38g; Fat 4g; Cholesterol 15mg; Sodium 440mg

Crunchy Cabbage Salad

Colorful vegetables mixed with crunchy noodles and a tangy dressing make a delightful salad.

Preparation time: 20 minutes (pictured on page 201)

Dressing

- ¼ cup vegetable oil
- 2 tablespoons sugar
- ¼ teaspoon salt
- ¼ teaspoon pepper
- 3 tablespoons red wine vinegar

Salad

- 3 cups shredded green cabbage
- 3 cups shredded red cabbage
- 2 medium (1 cup) carrots, shredded
- 3 tablespoons sliced green onions
- ¾ cup salted peanuts
- 1 (3-ounce) package uncooked chicken-flavored ramen noodle soup

In small bowl stir together all dressing ingredients; set aside.

In large bowl toss together green cabbage, red cabbage, carrots, green onions and ½ cup peanuts. Sprinkle dry soup seasoning packet over salad. Break noodles into small pieces; stir into salad. Pour dressing over salad; toss to coat. Sprinkle with remaining peanuts.

YIELD: 8 servings.

TIP. If softer noodles are preferred, salad can be prepared up to 4 hours ahead. Cover; refrigerate until ready to serve.

Nutrition Facts (1 serving): Calories 220; Protein 6g; Carbohydrate 18g; Fat 15g; Cholesterol 0mg; Sodium 440mg

Pineapple Pepper Dip

Assorted bell peppers, pineapple and fresh lime add color to this refreshing dip.

Preparation time: 30 minutes • Chilling time: 1 hour

1 cup chopped assorted
   peppers (green, red and/or
   yellow)
1 cup LAND O LAKES®
   Sour Cream
1 (8-ounce) package cream
   cheese, softened
1 (8-ounce) can crushed
   pineapple, well drained
2 tablespoons coarsely
   chopped fresh cilantro <u>or</u>
   parsley
2 tablespoons chopped green
   onion
2 teaspoons finely chopped
   seeded jalapeño pepper
1 teaspoon grated lime peel
1 teaspoon lime juice
1/8 teaspoon salt

Fresh vegetable sticks
   (pepper, celery, carrot,
   cucumber, etc.)
Tortilla chips

In small mixer bowl combine all ingredients <u>except</u> vegetable sticks and tortilla chips. Beat at medium speed, scraping bowl often, until well mixed (1 to 2 minutes). Cover; refrigerate at least 1 hour. Serve with fresh vegetable sticks or tortilla chips. **YIELD:** 3¹/4 cups.

Nutrition Facts (1 tablespoon): Calories 22; Protein 1g; Carbohydrate 1g; Fat 2g; Cholesterol 5mg; Sodium 25mg

Tomato & Cucumber *in* Vinaigrette

*Plump, ripe tomatoes and refreshing, crisp cucumbers pair up in
this fresh-from-the-garden salad.*

Preparation time: 30 minutes

Vinaigrette

- 1/3 cup olive <u>or</u> vegetable oil
- 1 tablespoon chopped fresh chives*
- 1 teaspoon chopped fresh mint leaves**
- 1/2 teaspoon sugar
- 1/4 teaspoon salt
- 1/4 teaspoon pepper
- 2 tablespoons red wine vinegar

Salad

- 6 Boston lettuce leaves, radicchio leaves <u>or</u> leaf lettuce leaves
- 3 ripe tomatoes, cut into 1/4-inch slices
- 1 medium cucumber, cut into 1/4-inch slices
- 1/2 cup sliced pitted ripe olives

In jar with tight-fitting lid combine all vinaigrette ingredients; shake well. Refrigerate until ready to serve.

On individual salad or dinner plates place <u>1</u> lettuce leaf. Arrange <u>3 to 4 slices</u> tomato and <u>4 to 5 slices</u> cucumber on each lettuce leaf. Sprinkle with olives. Just before serving, drizzle with vinaigrette.
YIELD: 6 servings.

*1 teaspoon dried chives can be substituted for 1 tablespoon chopped fresh chives.

**1/4 teaspoon dried mint leaves can be substituted for 1 teaspoon chopped fresh mint leaves.

Nutrition Facts (1 serving): Calories 140; Protein 1g; Carbohydrate 4g; Fat 14g; Cholesterol 0mg; Sodium 190mg

Potato, Cucumber & Onion Salad

This is a very colorful, refreshing vinaigrette potato salad, perfect for a summer supper.

Preparation time: 30 minutes • Standing time: 3 hours • Chilling time: 1 hour

Salad

2 large (3 cups) cucumbers, thinly sliced

1 small (1 cup) onion, thinly sliced

1 tablespoon salt

4 large (4 cups) russet potatoes, cooked, cut into 1-inch cubes

2 cups cherry tomato halves

Dressing

1/3 cup vegetable oil

1/3 cup white wine vinegar

1 teaspoon dried basil leaves

1/4 teaspoon coarsely ground pepper

In large bowl combine cucumber, onion and salt; mix well. Cover; let stand at room temperature, stirring occasionally, 3 to 4 hours.

Place cucumber mixture in strainer; drain. Press cucumbers with paper towels to remove excess moisture. Place cucumber mixture in large bowl. Add potatoes and cherry tomatoes.

In small bowl combine all dressing ingredients. Pour over cucumber mixture; toss to coat well. Cover; refrigerate at least 1 hour to blend flavors. **YIELD:** 8 servings.

Nutrition Facts (1 serving): Calories 160; Protein 2g; Carbohydrate 18g; Fat 9g; Cholesterol 0mg; Sodium 280mg

Stove Top Spicy Baked Beans

Salsa adds a southwestern flair to these stove top baked beans.

Preparation time: 20 minutes • Cooking time: 48 minutes

3 (16-ounce) cans baked beans

1 (16-ounce) jar (2 cups) medium salsa

1 pound hickory smoked bacon, cooked, crumbled

1 cup chopped red onion

1/4 cup firmly packed brown sugar

1/4 cup chopped fresh parsley

2 tablespoons stone ground mustard

2 tablespoons light molasses

1 teaspoon finely chopped fresh garlic

2 tablespoons red wine vinegar

In 3-quart saucepan combine all ingredients. Cook over medium heat, stirring occasionally, until beans come to a full boil (8 to 12 minutes). Reduce heat to low; continue cooking, stirring occasionally, until flavors blend (40 to 45 minutes). **YIELD:** 12 servings.

Nutrition Facts (1 serving): Calories 230; Protein 9g; Carbohydrate 33g; Fat 7g; Cholesterol 15mg; Sodium 930mg

Shrimp Dilled Deviled Eggs

Place these shrimp and dill-seasoned deviled eggs in a plastic food wrap lined egg carton for easy carrying to a picnic or barbecue.

Preparation time: 30 minutes (pictured on page 211)

6 hard-cooked eggs, peeled
1/4 cup mayonnaise
1 (4¹/₄-ounce) can deveined medium shrimp, rinsed, drained, <u>reserve 12 shrimp</u>
2 tablespoons chopped green onions
1 tablespoon chopped fresh dill*
1/8 teaspoon pepper
2 teaspoons country-style Dijon mustard
1 tablespoon lime juice
1/4 teaspoon hot pepper sauce

Fresh dill

Cut eggs crosswise in half. Remove yolks from egg whites; set egg whites aside. Place cooked egg yolks in medium bowl; mash with fork. Add mayonnaise, shrimp, onions, 1 tablespoon dill, pepper, mustard, lime juice and hot pepper sauce to egg yolks; stir to blend. Spoon about 1 tablespoon egg yolk mixture into each egg white; garnish with reserved shrimp and sprig of dill. Cover; refrigerate. **YIELD:** 1 dozen.

* 1 teaspoon dried dill weed can be substituted for 1 tablespoon chopped fresh dill.

Nutrition Facts (1 egg): Calories 90; Protein 5g; Carbohydrate 1g; Fat 7g; Cholesterol 125mg; Sodium 85mg

Corn *on the* Cob *with* Seasoned Butters

*This corn on the cob tastes great with grilled hamburgers,
baked beans and relishes.*

Preparation time: 30 minutes • Grilling time: 20 minutes (pictured on page 211)

1/2 cup LAND O LAKES®
   Butter, softened

Dill Butter
   2 teaspoons dried chives
   1 teaspoon dried dill weed
   1 teaspoon lemon juice

Italian Butter
   1/4 teaspoon dried basil leaves
   1/4 teaspoon dried oregano
      leaves
   1/4 teaspoon garlic salt

Horseradish Parsley Butter
   1 tablespoon chopped fresh
      parsley
   1/4 teaspoon salt
   1/8 teaspoon pepper
   2 teaspoons prepared
      horseradish

Sesame Mustard Butter
   2 tablespoons sesame seed,
      toasted
   1/4 teaspoon salt
   1/4 teaspoon dry mustard
   1/8 teaspoon pepper

   Corn on the cob, husked

In small mixer bowl combine butter and all ingredients for desired seasoned butter. Beat at medium speed, scraping bowl often, until light and fluffy (1 to 2 minutes). Serve butter at room temperature with hot sweet corn. **YIELD:** 1/2 cup butter.

Grilling Directions: Prepare grill; heat until coals are ash white. Spread about 1 tablespoon desired seasoned butter evenly over each ear of corn. Wrap each ear of corn tightly in heavy-duty double thickness aluminum foil; seal well. Place on grill directly over coals. Grill, turning every 5 minutes, until tender (20 to 25 minutes).

Stove Top Directions: In 5-quart Dutch oven bring enough water to a full boil to cover corn. Add corn; return water to full boil. Cover; continue boiling until corn is tender (5 to 8 minutes).

Microwave Directions: In ungreased 12x8-inch baking dish combine 1/4 cup water and 4 ears of corn. Cover with plastic food wrap; microwave on HIGH, rearranging corn every 3 minutes, until corn is tender (10 to 11 minutes). Let stand 1 minutes; drain.

*Nutrition Facts (1 teaspoon Dill Butter only): Calories 35; Protein 0g; Carbohydrate 0g; Fat 4g;
Cholesterol 10mg; Sodium 40mg*

Grilled Sourdough Bread
with Garden Tomatoes

This bread uses the season's finest garden ripened tomatoes and fresh sweet basil leaves.

Preparation time: 30 minutes • Grilling time: 3 minutes

1/4 cup LAND O LAKES® Butter

2 tablespoons chopped shallots or onion

1/2 teaspoon finely chopped fresh garlic

4 (1/2-inch) slices round sourdough bread

1/4 cup torn fresh basil leaves

2 medium ripe tomatoes, each cut into 6 slices

2 teaspoons red wine vinegar
   Salt and coarsely ground pepper

Prepare grill; heat until coals are ash white.

Meanwhile, in 1-quart saucepan melt butter until sizzling; stir in shallots and garlic. Cook over medium heat, stirring occasionally, until shallots are tender (1 to 2 minutes). Place bread slices on grill. Grill until toasted (2 to 3 minutes). Turn; brush each bread slice with butter mixture. Sprinkle with basil; top each bread slice with 3 tomato slices. Sprinkle each with 1/2 teaspoon vinegar; season with salt and pepper. Continue grilling until bread is lightly browned (1 to 2 minutes). **YIELD:** 4 servings.

Nutrition Facts (1 serving): Calories 220; Protein 4g; Carbohydrate 22g; Fat 13g; Cholesterol 30mg; Sodium 330mg

Grilled Fruit Kabobs
with Coconut Cream Dip

*These fresh fruit kabobs are delicious when served
with a tropical coconut cream.*

Preparation time: 30 minutes • Marinating time: 1 hour • Grilling time: 5 minutes

Kabobs

1 (20-ounce) can chunk
    pineapple in juice, drained,
    <u>reserve juice</u>

2/3 cup honey

1 red apple, cut into 1-inch
    pieces

1 green apple, cut into 1-inch
    pieces

2 bananas, cut into 1-inch
    pieces

12 to 16 maraschino cherries

8 (8-inch) wooden skewers,
    soaked in water

Dip

1 cup LAND O LAKES®
    Sour Cream

1/2 cup flaked coconut, toasted

1/2 teaspoon vanilla

In large plastic food bag place $^1/2$ cup reserved pineapple juice and honey; add pineapple and all remaining kabob ingredients <u>except</u> wooden skewers. Tightly seal bag. Turn bag several times to coat fruit well. Place in 13x9-inch pan. Refrigerate at least 1 hour to blend flavors.

Meanwhile, <u>prepare grill</u> placing coals to one side; heat until coals are ash white. Make aluminum foil drip pan; place opposite coals. To assemble kabobs on wooden skewers alternately thread fruit; <u>reserve juice and honey mixture</u>. In small bowl stir together $^1/4$ cup reserved juice and honey mixture, sour cream, coconut and vanilla; set aside.

Place kabobs on grill over drip pan. Cover; grill kabobs, turning occasionally, until heated through (5 to 8 minutes). Serve with dip.
YIELD: 8 servings ($1^1/2$ cups dip).

*Nutrition Facts (1 serving): Calories 180; Protein 2g; Carbohydrate 37g; Fat 4g;
Cholesterol 5mg; Sodium 35mg*

Lemon Zest Dressing *over* Fresh Fruit

A light lemonade dressing is drizzled over sliced pineapple, strawberries and kiwi.

Preparation time: 20 minutes

1/4 cup lemon juice

2 teaspoons sugar

1 teaspoon grated lemon peel

6 (1/4-inch) slices fresh pineapple, peeled, cored

1 pint strawberries, hulled, sliced 1/4-inch

1 kiwi fruit, peeled, sliced 1/8-inch, cut in half

In small bowl stir together lemon juice, sugar and lemon peel. On individual salad plates place <u>1 slice</u> pineapple; divide strawberries and kiwi evenly between salad plates. Spoon about <u>2 teaspoons</u> dressing over each serving. **YIELD:** 6 servings.

TIP: Dressing can be used on your favorite combination of fruits.

Nutrition Facts (1 serving): Calories 70; Protein 1g; Carbohydrate 18g; Fat 1g; Cholesterol 0mg; Sodium 4mg

Sparkling Pink Lemonade

*Spending a hot day on the front porch is just not the same without homemade lemonade–
especially when it's sparkling pink!*

Preparation time: 10 minutes • Chilling time: 30 minutes

1¹/₂ cups sugar

1¹/₂ cups (6 lemons) freshly
    squeezed lemon juice

1 quart (4 cups) club soda,
    chilled*

4 teaspoons grenadine
    syrup**

  6-inch wooden skewers

  Fresh fruit pieces
    (strawberries, melon balls,
    pineapple chunks, etc.)

In 2-quart pitcher combine sugar and lemon juice. Stir well; refrigerate at least 30 minutes.

Just before serving, add club soda. Stir in grenadine syrup. On 6-inch wooden skewers, thread fruit pieces to make kabobs. Place kabobs in glasses; add ice. Pour in lemonade. **YIELD:** 6 servings.

*1 quart (4 cups) water can be substituted for club soda.

**4 to 6 drops red food coloring can be substituted for grenadine syrup.

*Nutrition Facts (1 serving): Calories 220; Protein 0g; Carbohydrate 58g; Fat 0g;
Cholesterol 0mg; Sodium 35mg*

Index

Metric & U.S. Measurements

Cooking Measure Equivalents

Small Liquid & Dry Measure (volume)	
1/4 teaspoon	1 mL
1/2 teaspoon	2 mL
1 teaspoon	5 mL
1 tablespoon	15 mL
1 coffee measure	25 mL

Large Liquid & Dry Measure (volume)	
1/4 cup	50 mL
1/2 cup	125 mL
1 cup	250 mL
2 cups	500 mL
4 cups	1 Liter

Liquid Measure (volume)	
1 fl. oz.	30 mL
2 fl. oz.	60 mL
3 fl. oz.	100 mL
4 fl. oz.	125 mL
6 fl. oz.	200 mL
8 fl. oz.	250 mL

Dry Measure (weight)	
1 oz.	30 g
1/2 lb. (8 oz.)	220 g
1 lb. (16 oz.)	450 g
2 lbs. (32 oz.)	900 g

Oven Temperature Guide

Celsius	80	100	110	120	140	150	160	180	190	200	220	230	240	260
Fahrenheit	170	200	225	250	275	300	325	350	375	400	425	450	475	500

Cookware Sizes

	Metric Volume	Closest Size in Centimeters	Closest Size in Inches or Volume
Pie Plate	1L	22 x 3 cm	9 x 1 1/4 inch
Skillets or Fry Pans	—	25 x 25 x 5 cm	10 x 10 x 2 inch
	—	30 x 30 x 5 cm	12 x 12 x 2 inch
	—	33 x 33 x 5 cm	13 x 13 x 2 inch
Casseroles	500 mL	—	20 fl. oz.
	750 mL	—	24 fl. oz.
	1 L	—	1 qt.
	1.5 L	—	1 1/2 qt.
	2 L	—	2 qt.
	2.5 L	—	2 1/2 qt.
	3 L	—	3 qt.
	4 L	—	4 qt.